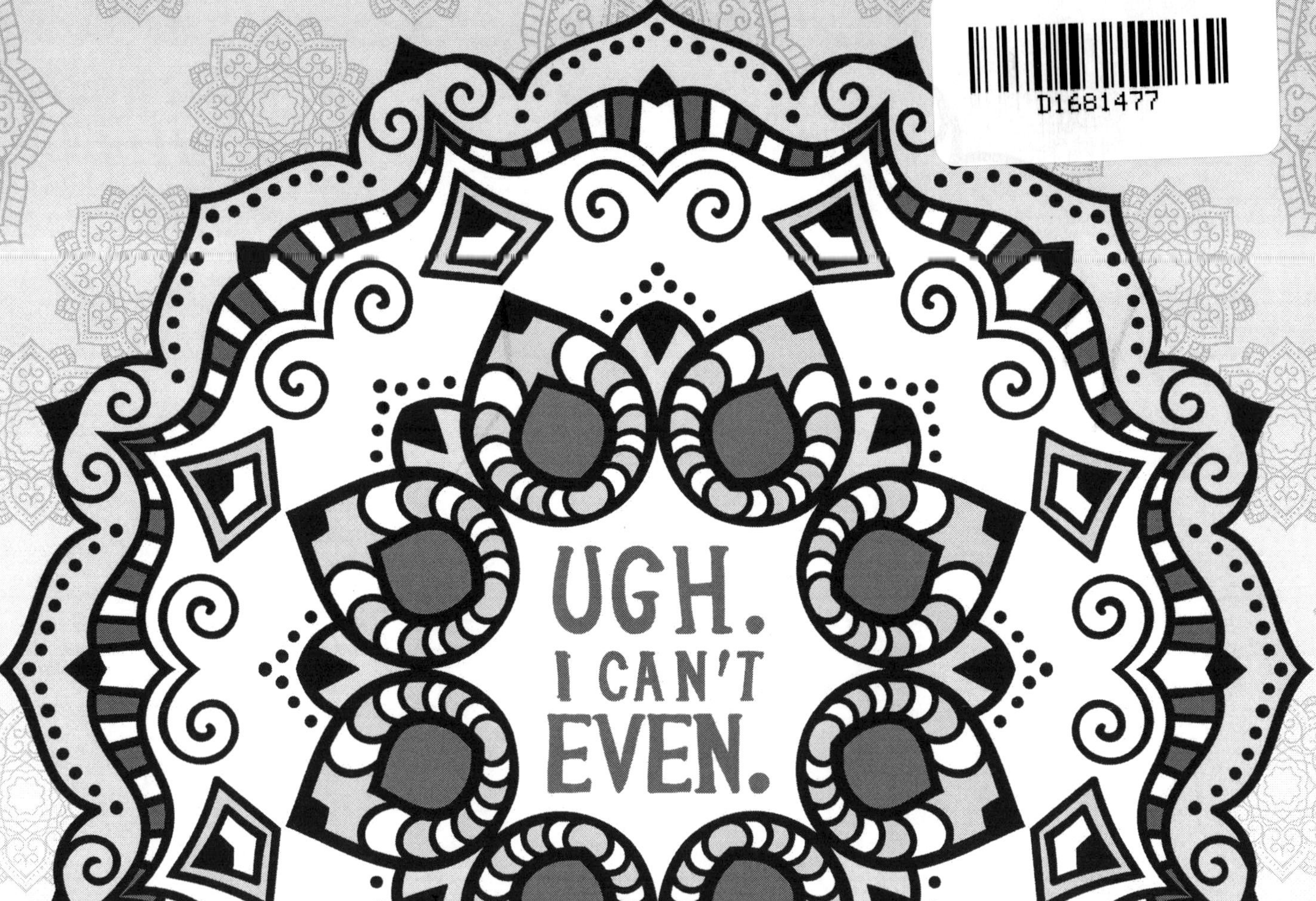
UGH.
I CAN'T
EVEN.

MANDALAS? MEH.

A SNARKY ADULT COLORING BOOK

Papeterie Bleu

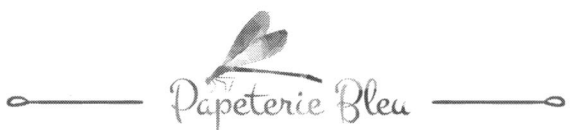

THE SWEAR WORD ADULT COLORING BOOK HAS EVOLVED BEYOND THE SWEARY WORDS WITH THE USE OF SASSY SNARKY SARCASM IN LIEU OF SAUCY SWEARY SWEARS

Copyright © 2016 Papeterie Bleu
All rights reserved.

ISBN-13: 978-1530887873
ISBN-10: 1530887879

" SOME PEOPLE JUST NEED A HIGH-FIVE. IN THE FACE. WITH A CHAIR."

-THE SNARKY MANDALA

Just because Donald Trump's campaign speeches have inspired an entire line of Swear Word Adult Coloring Books, doesn't mean we need another coloring book with the F-bomb on the cover. Let's combine that anger and negativity, add a cup of sarcasm, a dash of passive aggressiveness, and a sprinkle of sass. Let this simmer on low, deep in your brain, for 20 minutes (or until it glows bright red). Your SNARK is now ready. As with revenge, this dish is best served cold. Popular recipients of this dish include: your boss, your mother in law, your ex, and of course, any telephone customer service representative.
Happy Coloring? *Shrug.*

@papeteriebleu

Papeterie Bleu

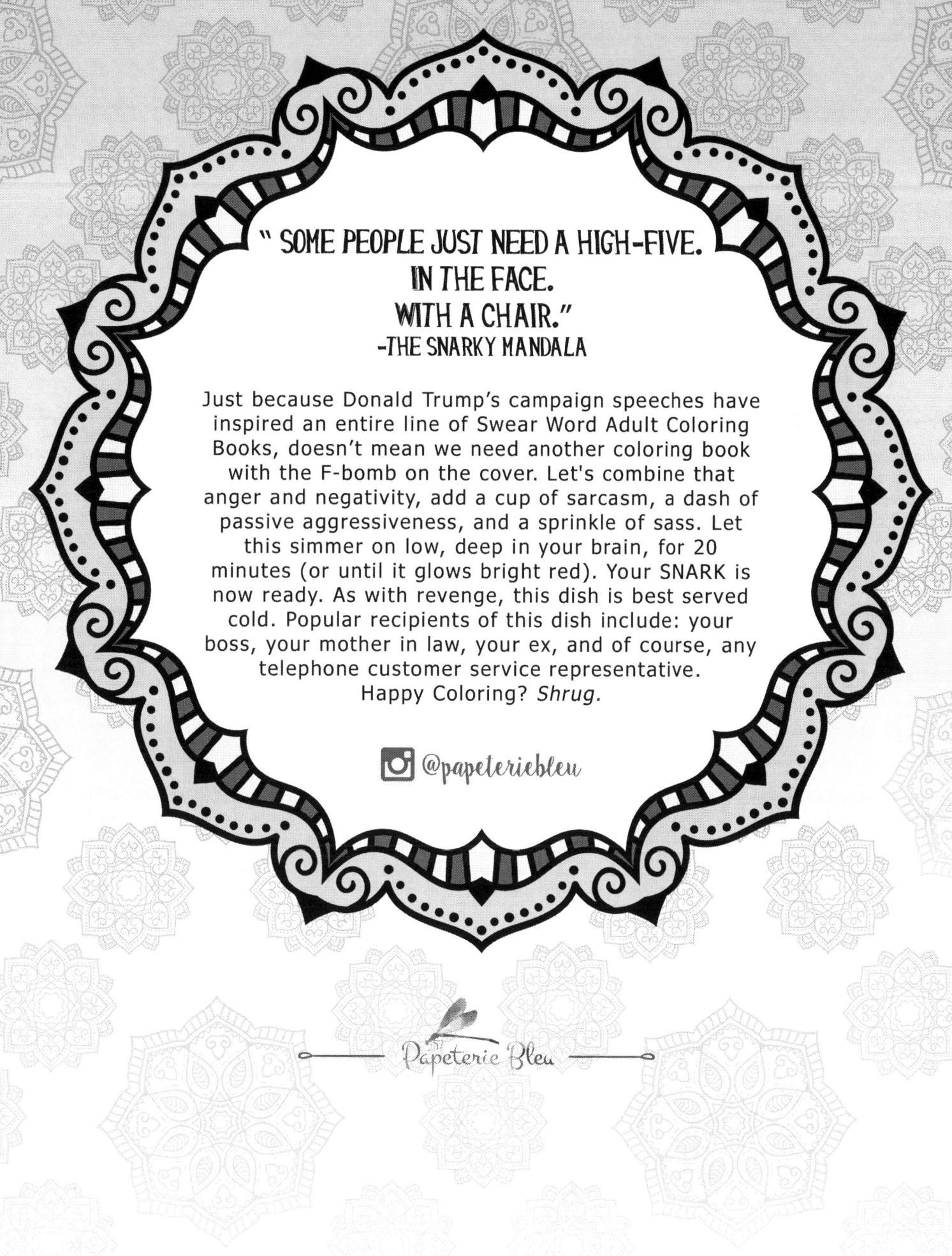

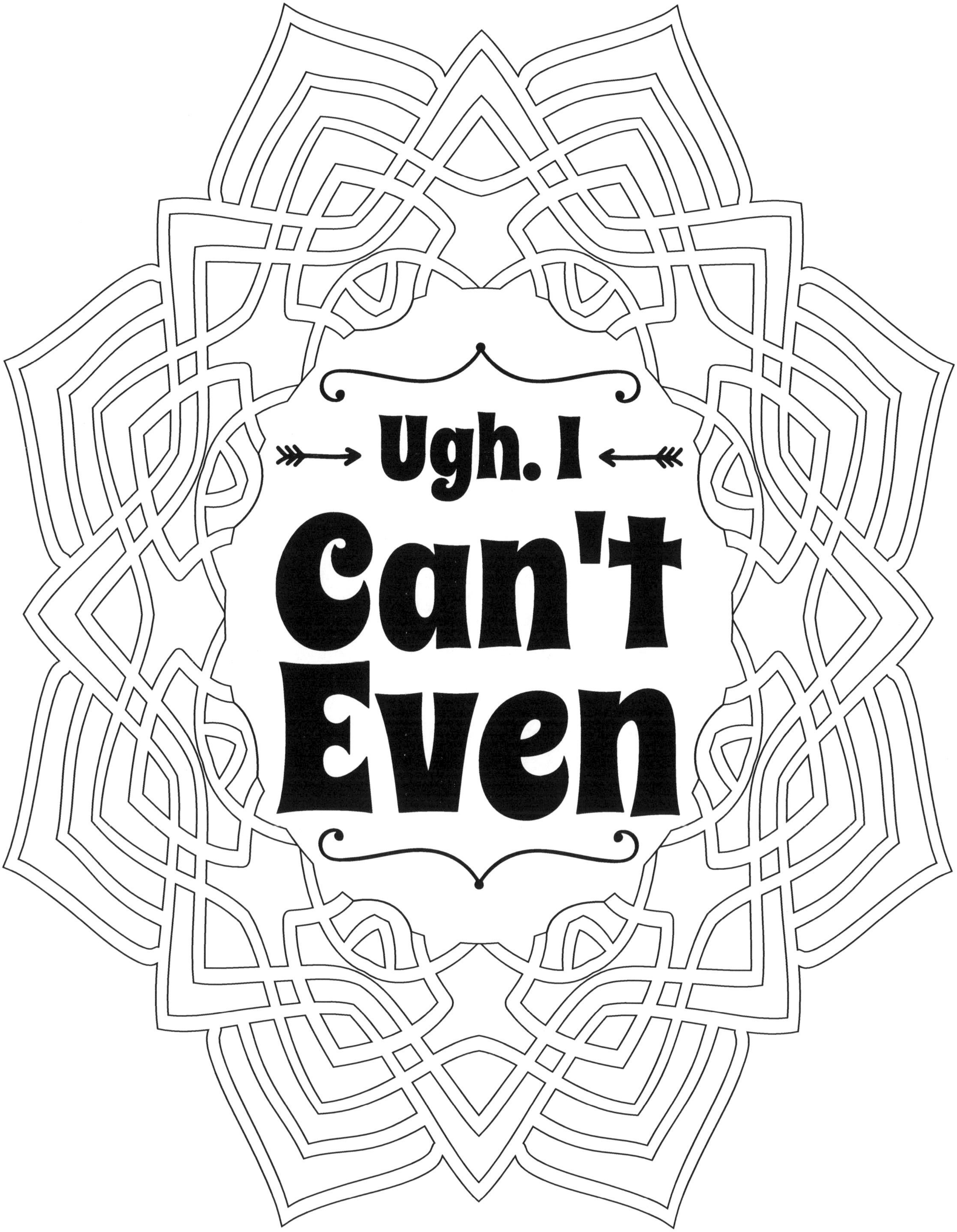
Ugh. I
Can't
Even

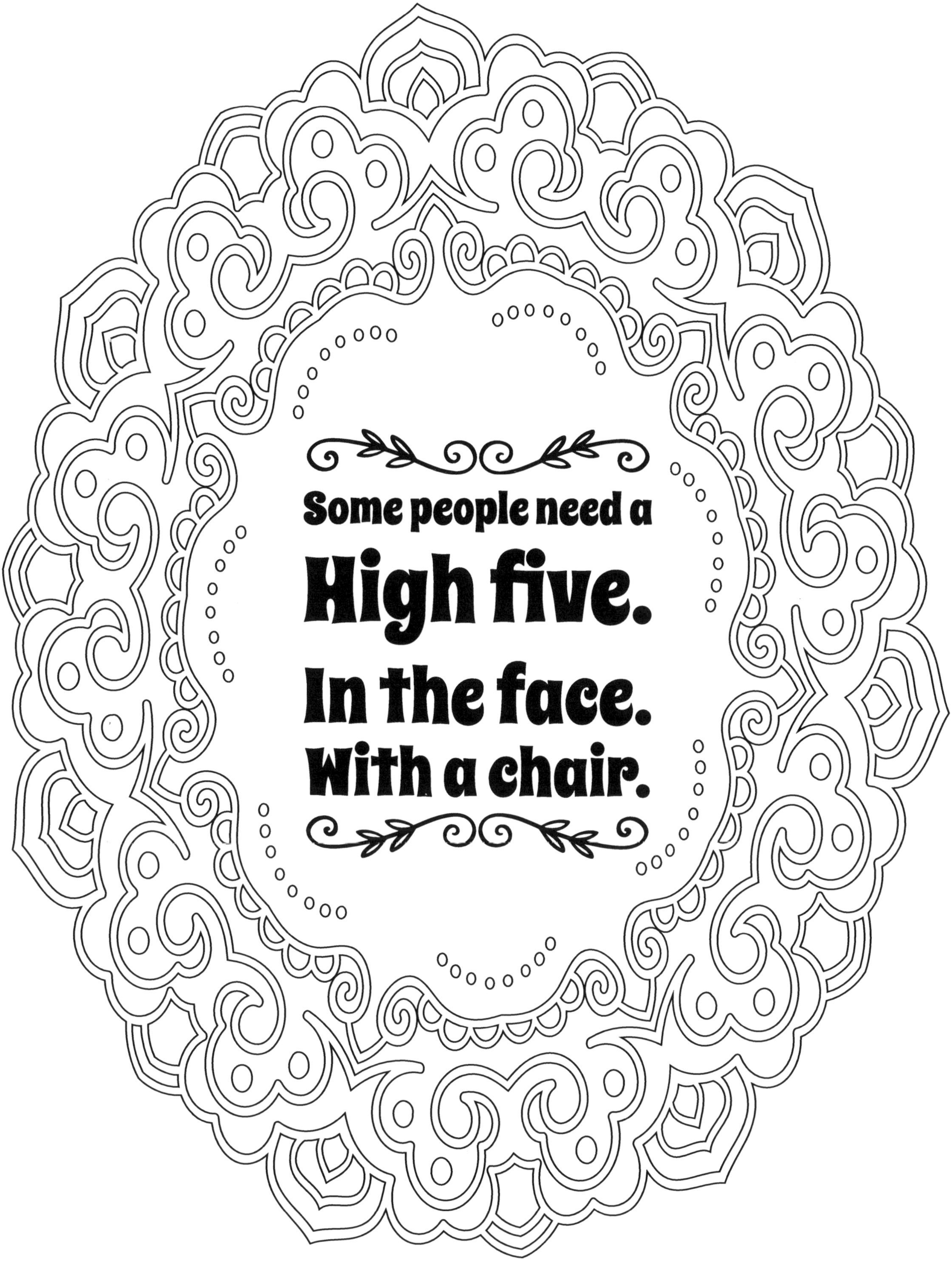
Some people need a
High five.
In the face.
With a chair.

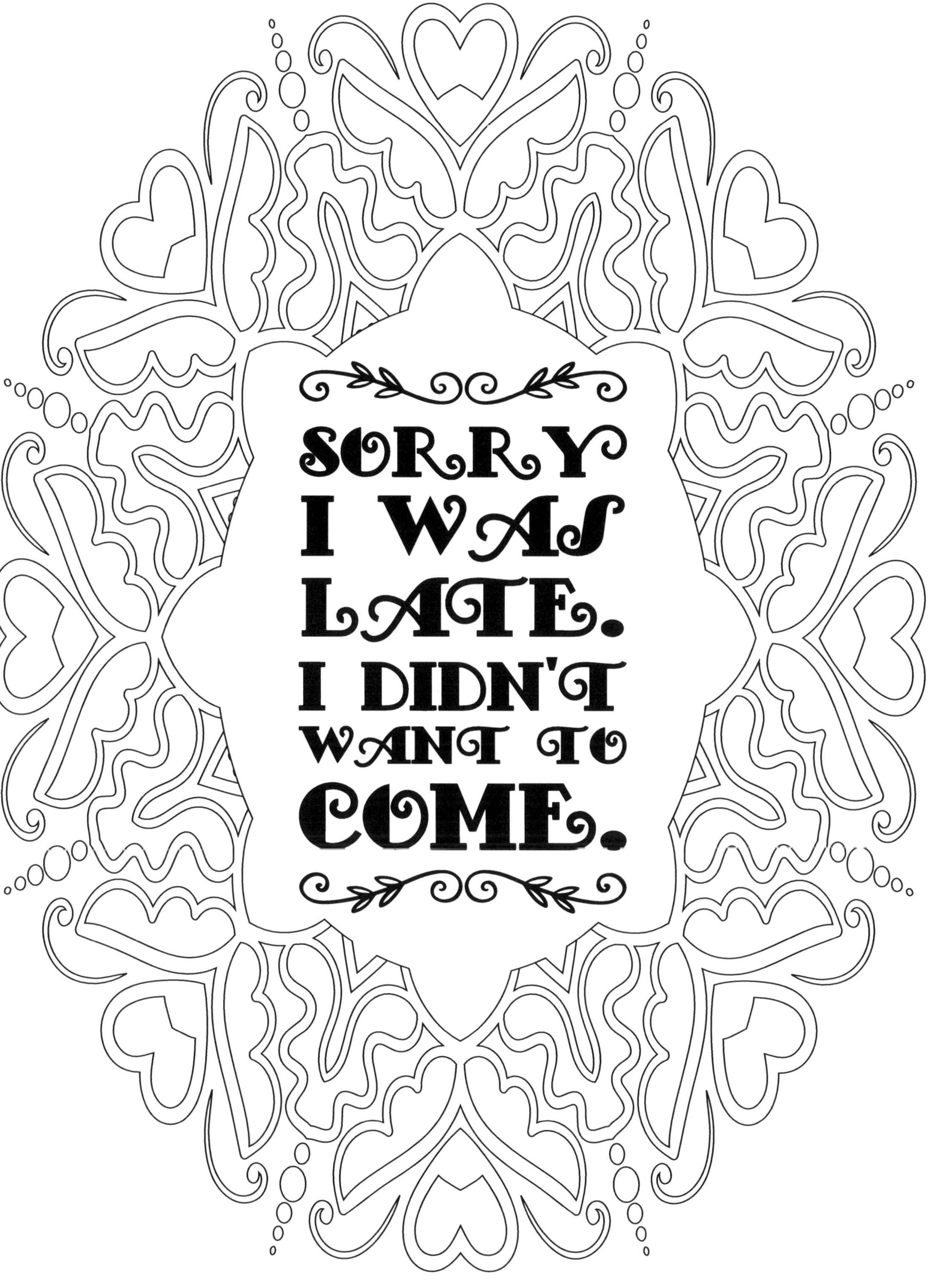
SORRY
I WAS
LATE.
I DIDN'T
WANT TO
COME.

EXERCISE WOULD BE SO MUCH MORE REWARDING IF CALORIES SCREAMED WHILE YOU BURNED THEM.

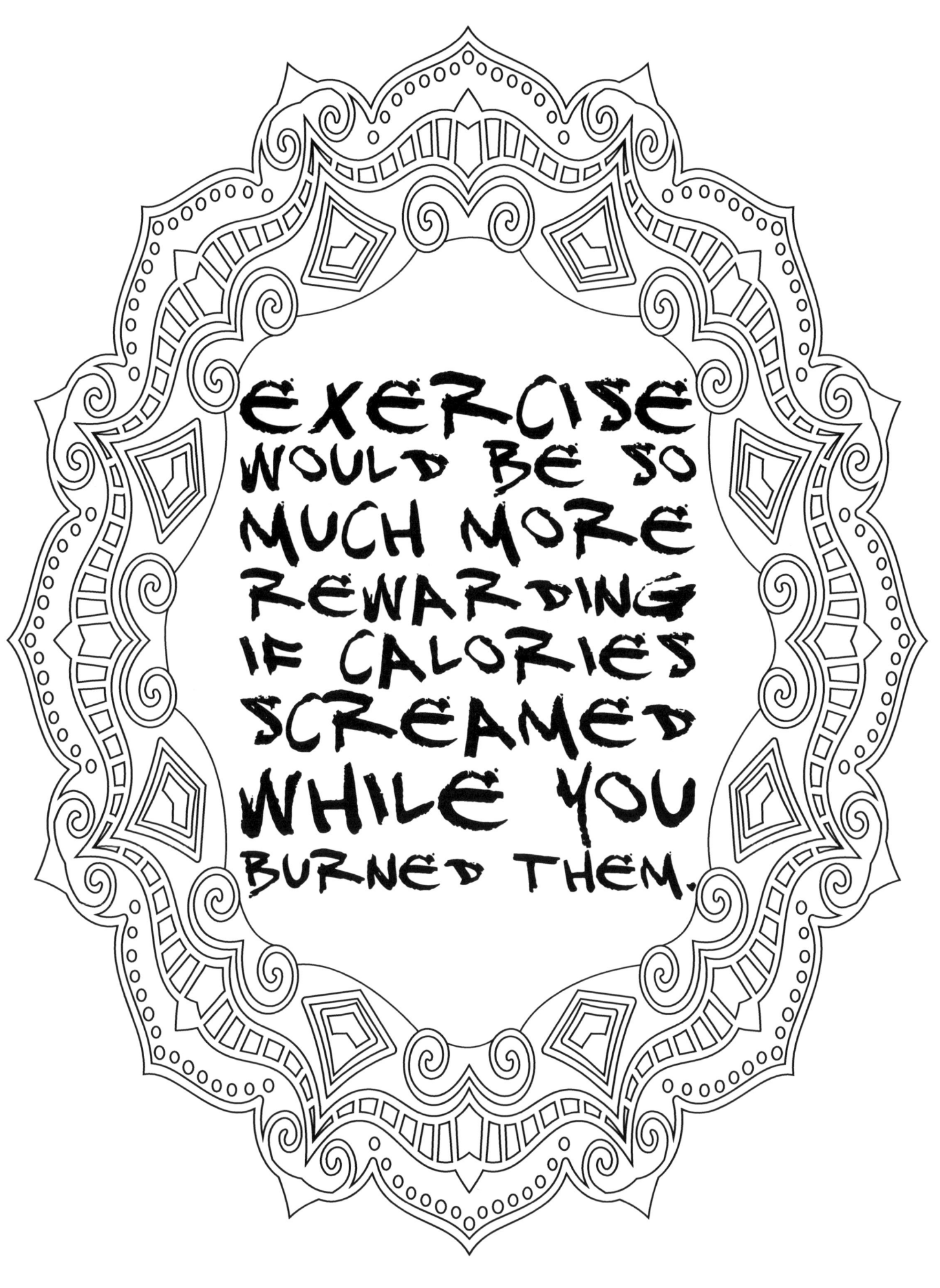

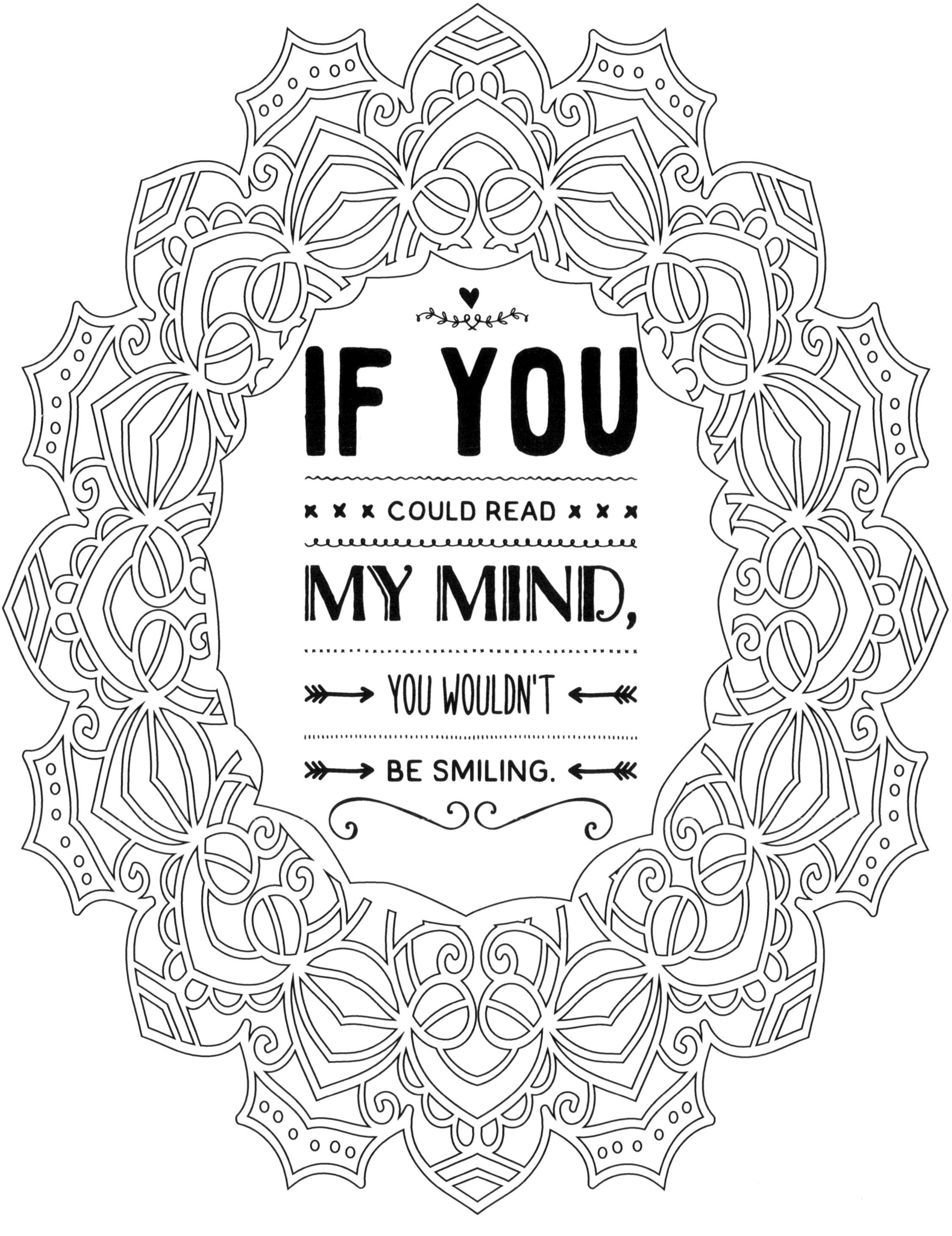
IF YOU
COULD READ
MY MIND,
YOU WOULDN'T
BE SMILING.

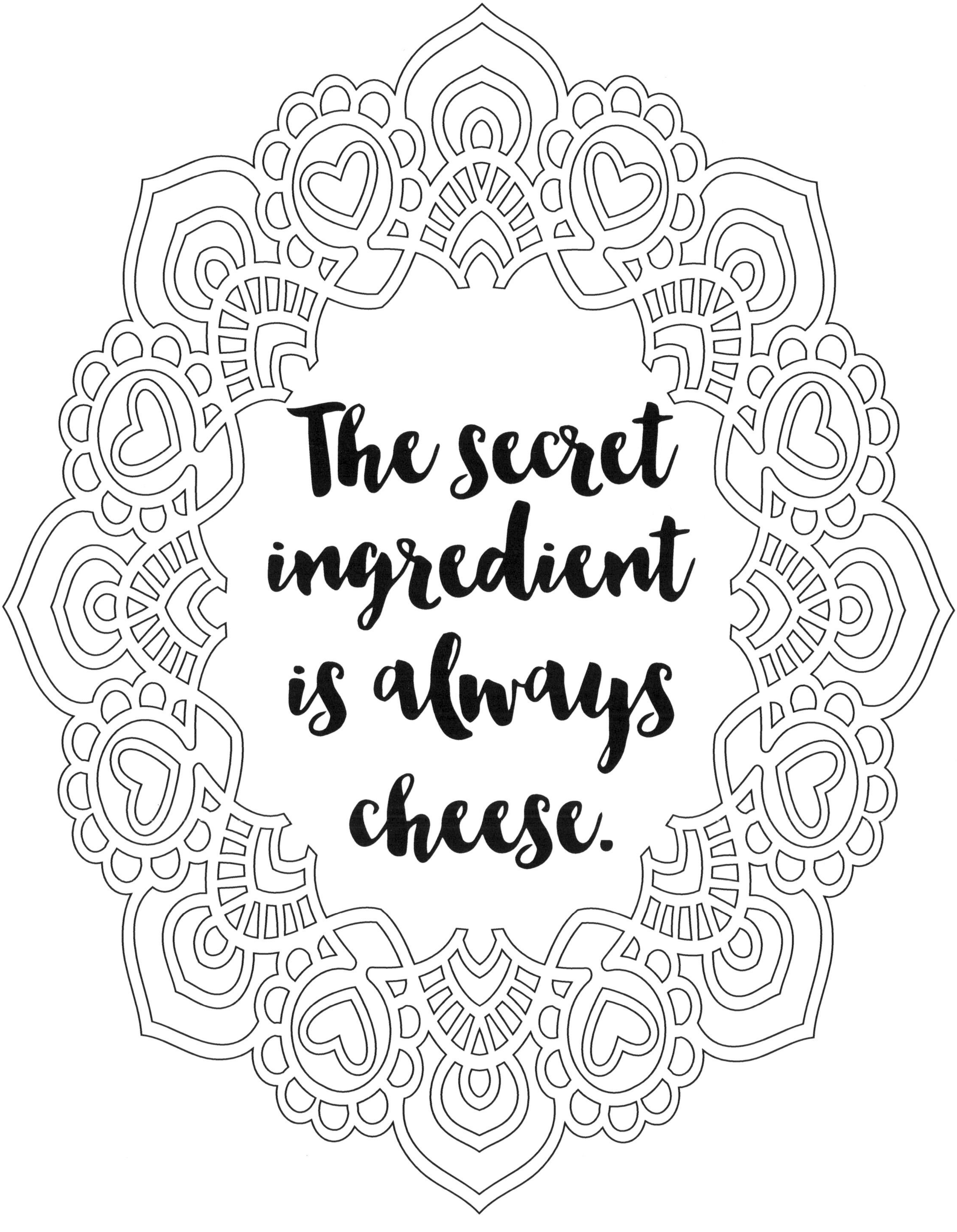
The secret ingredient is always cheese.

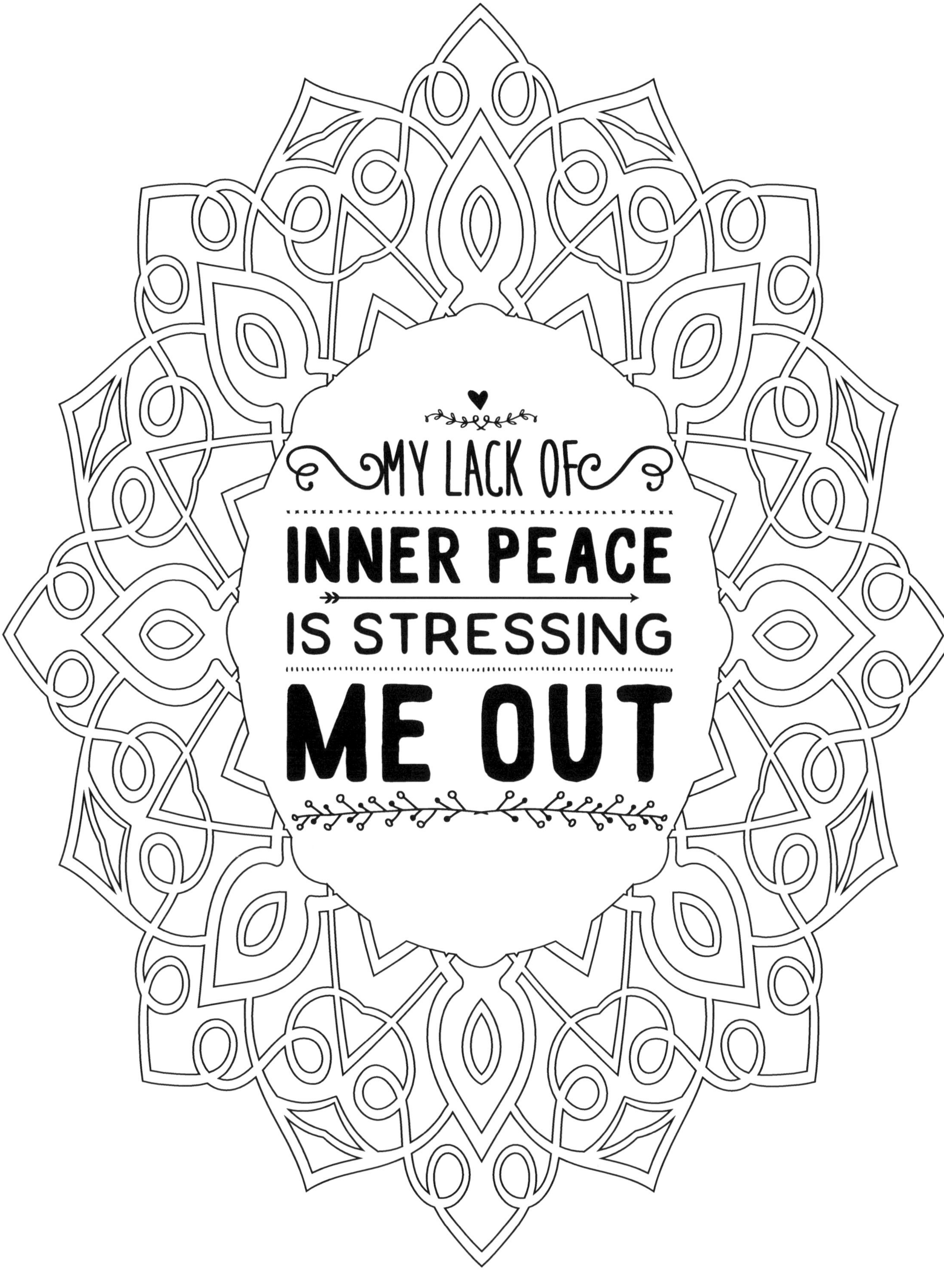
MY LACK OF
INNER PEACE
IS STRESSING
ME OUT

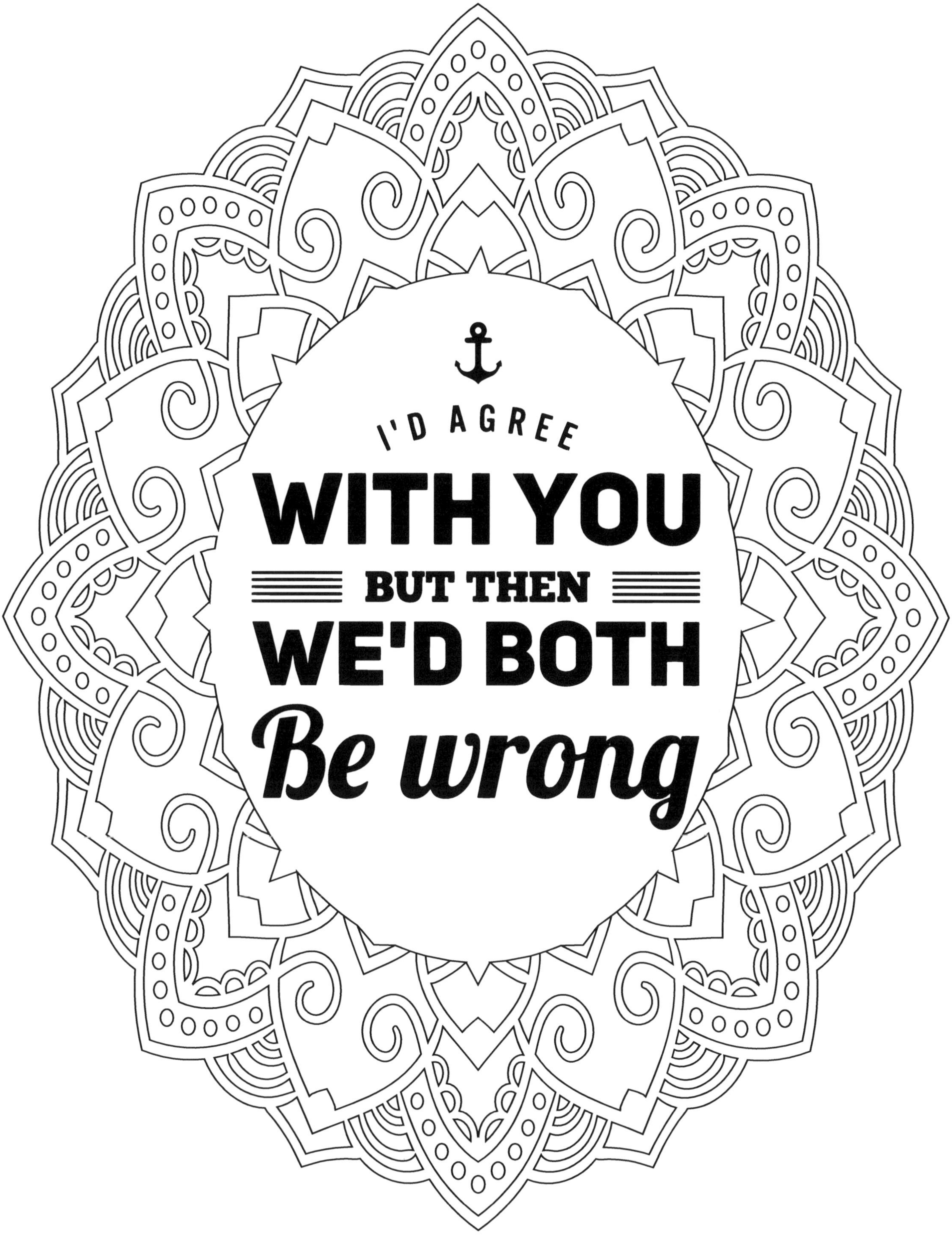
I'D AGREE
WITH YOU
BUT THEN
WE'D BOTH
Be wrong

ME? CRAZY?

I SHOULD GET DOWN OFF THIS UNICORN AND SLAP YOU!

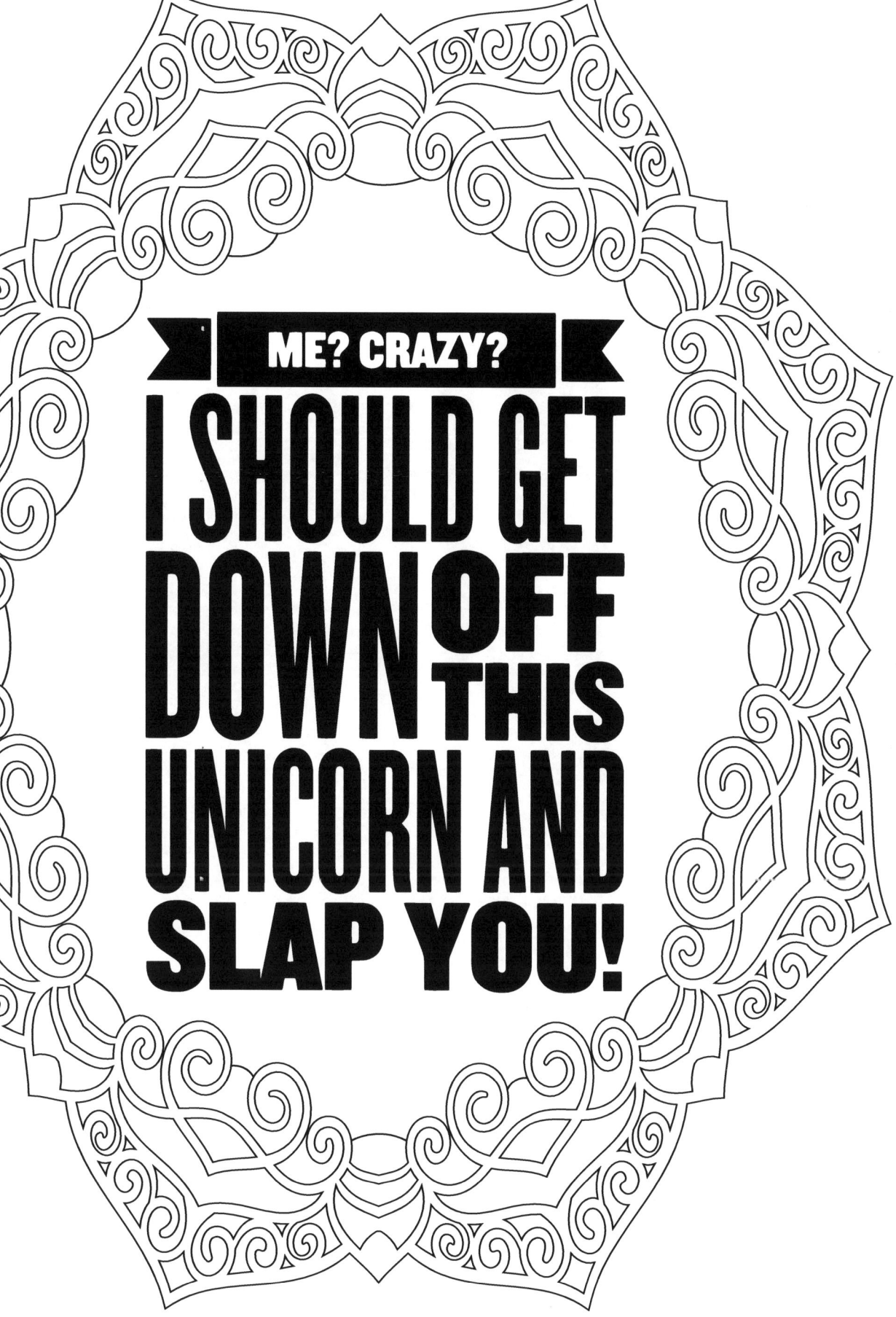

I found your nose.
It was in my business

again.

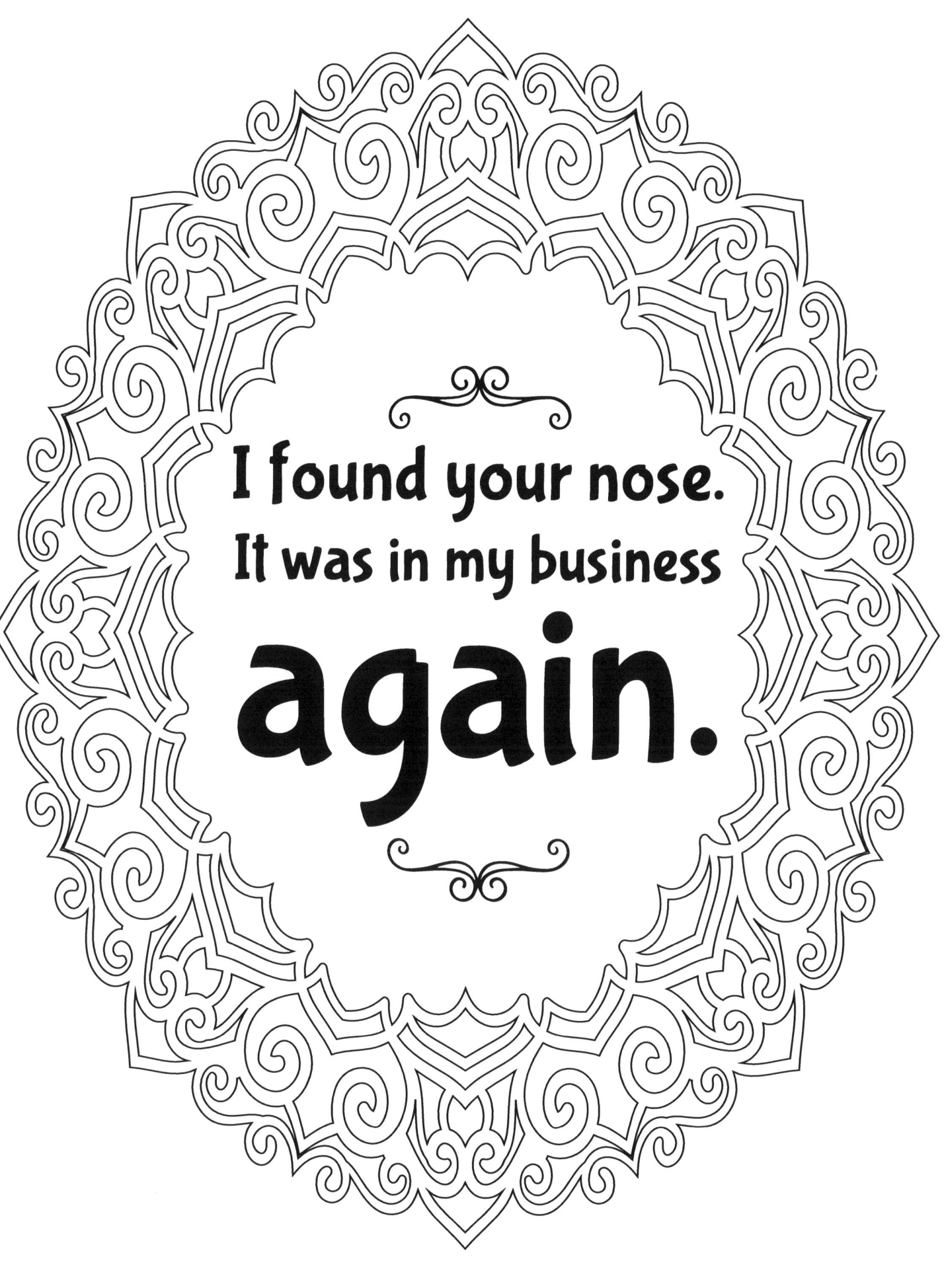

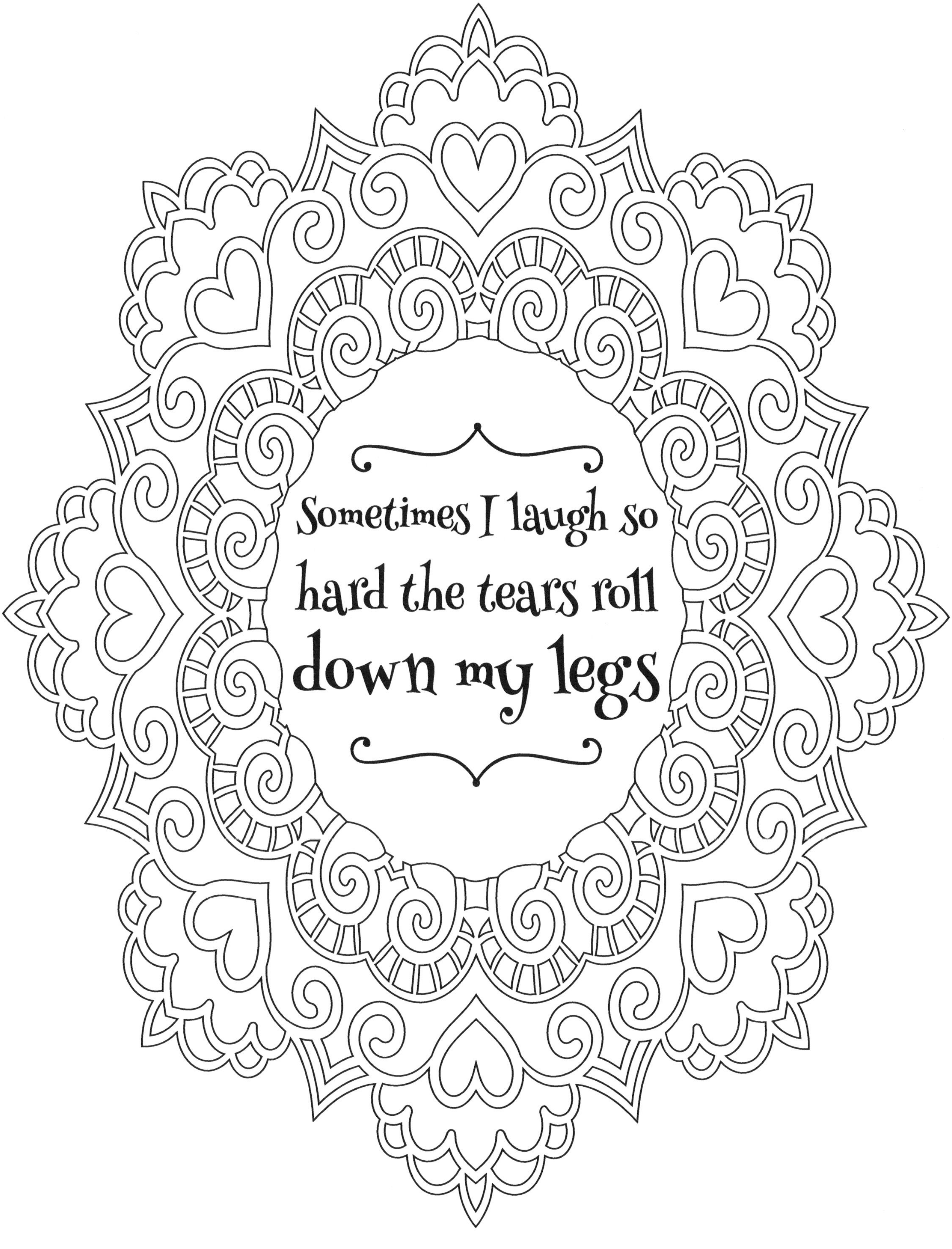
Sometimes I laugh so
hard the tears roll
down my legs

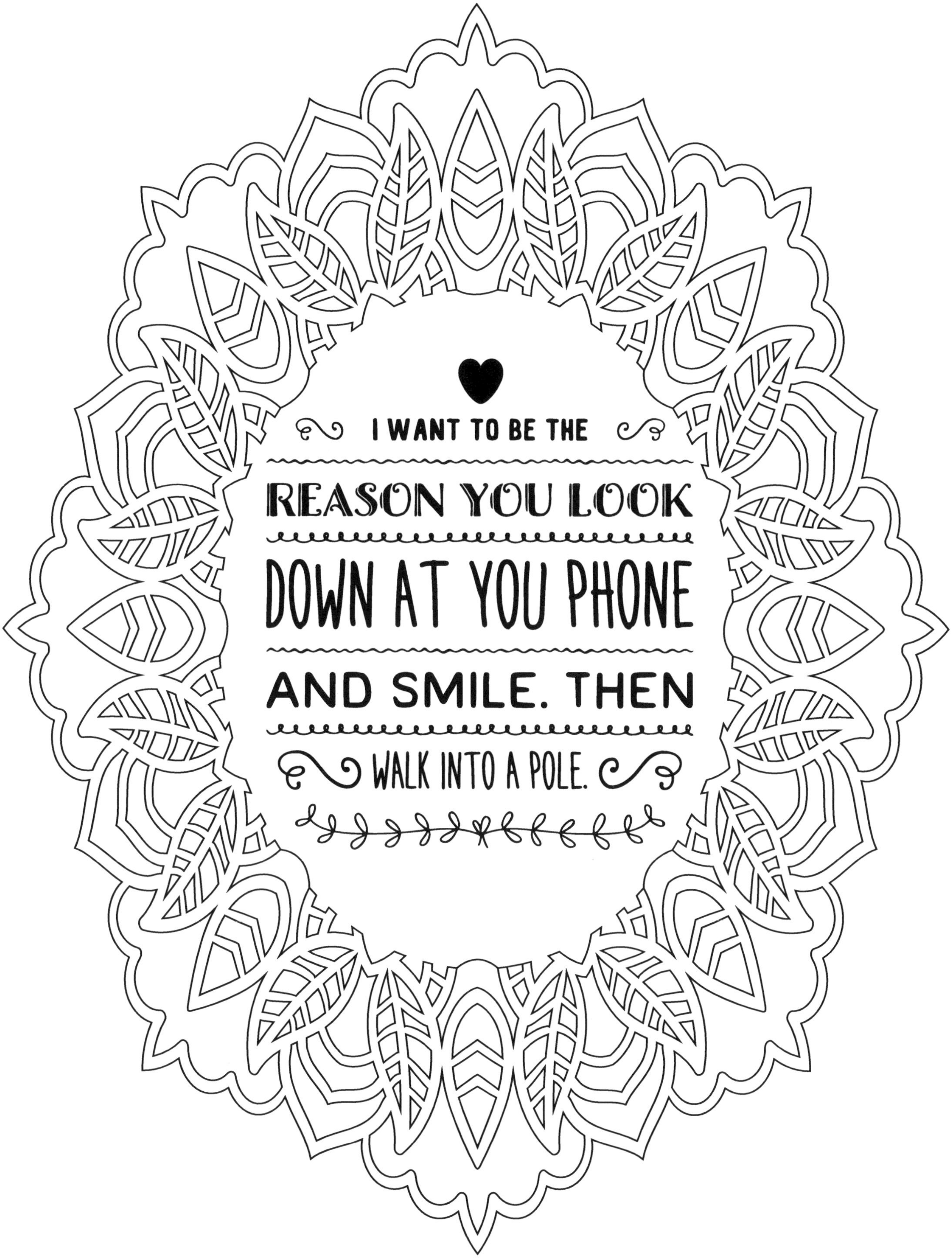
I WANT TO BE THE
REASON YOU LOOK
DOWN AT YOU PHONE
AND SMILE. THEN
WALK INTO A POLE.

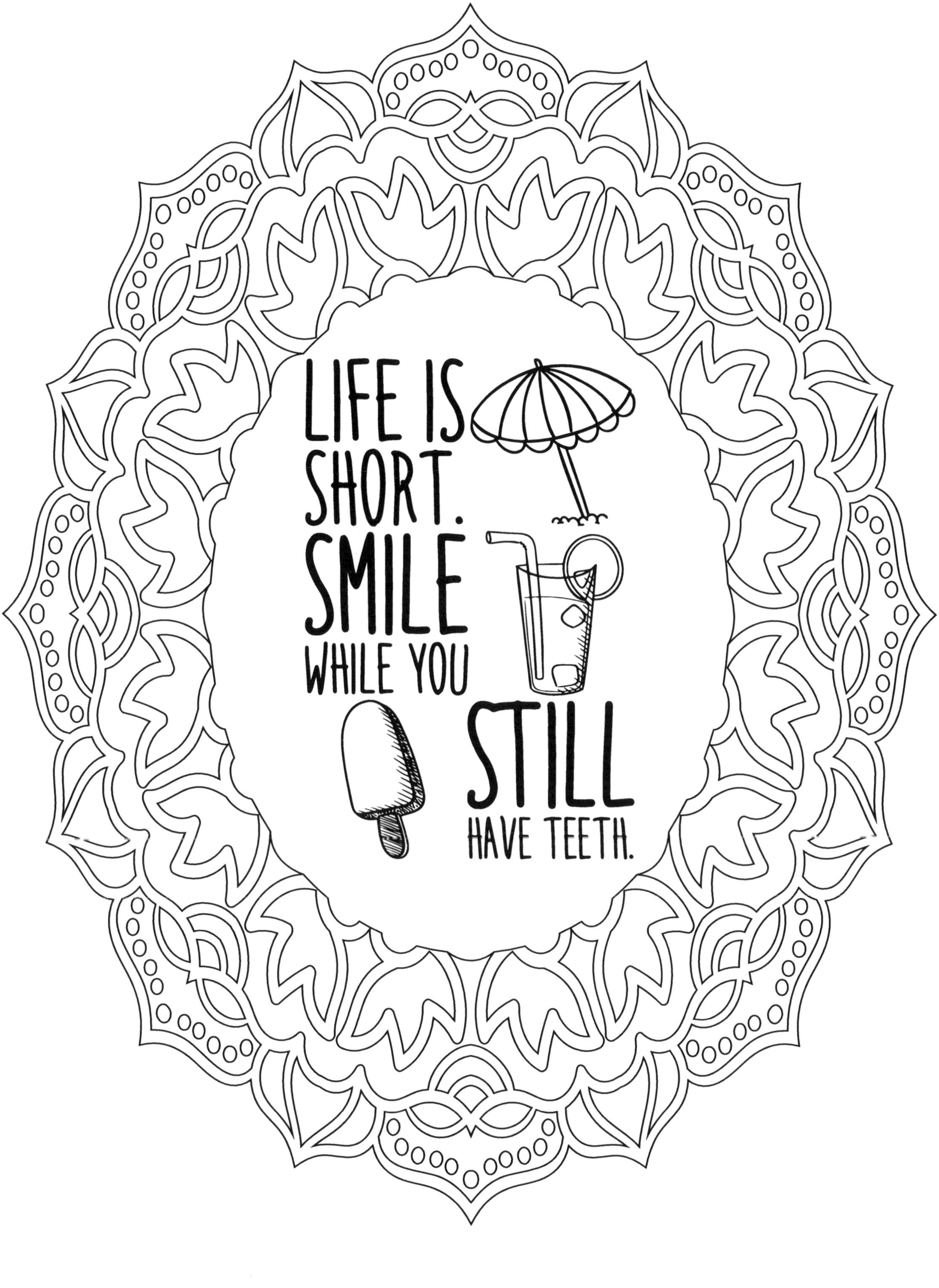
LIFE IS
SHORT.
SMILE
WHILE YOU
STILL
HAVE TEETH.

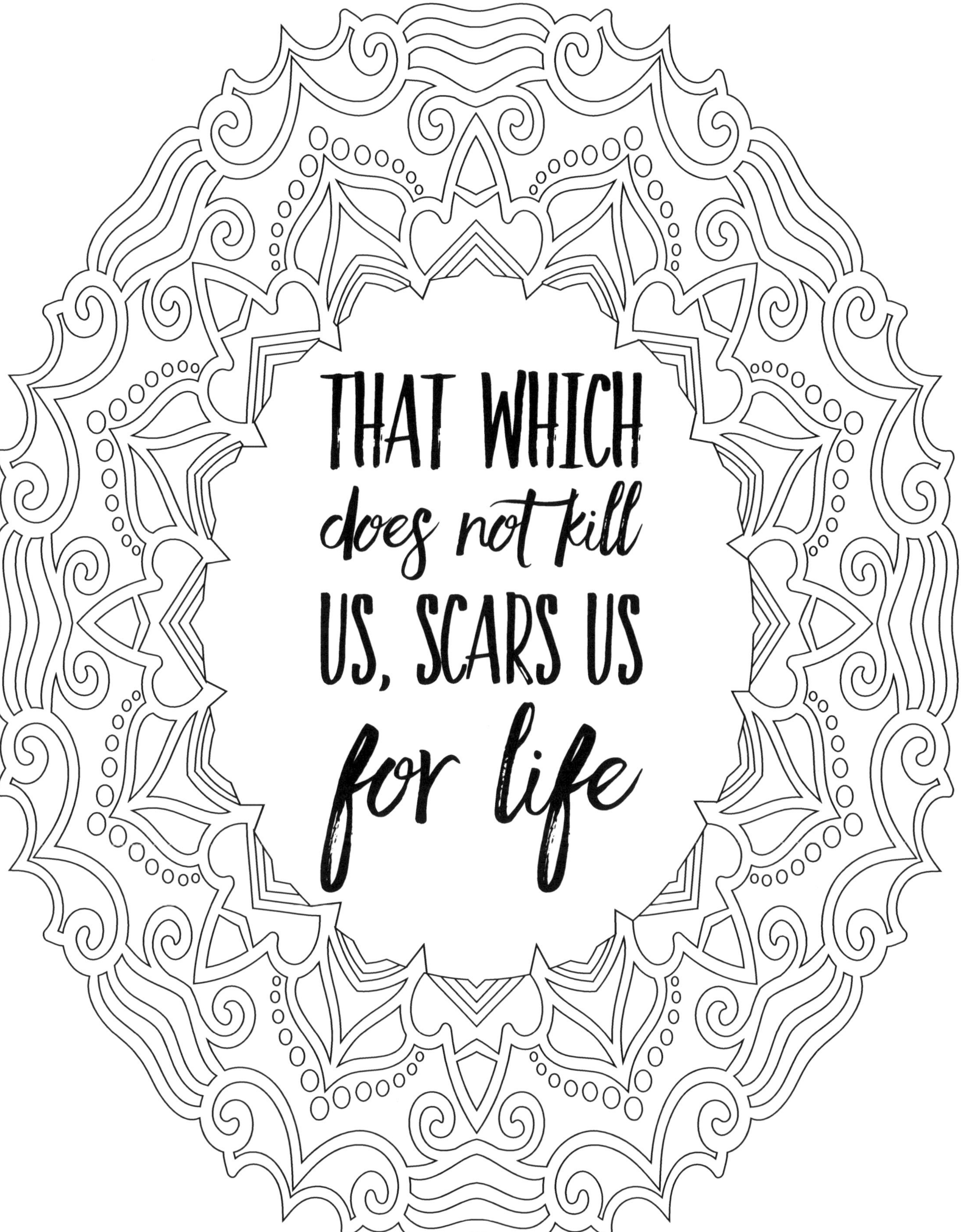
THAT WHICH
does not kill
US, SCARS US
for life

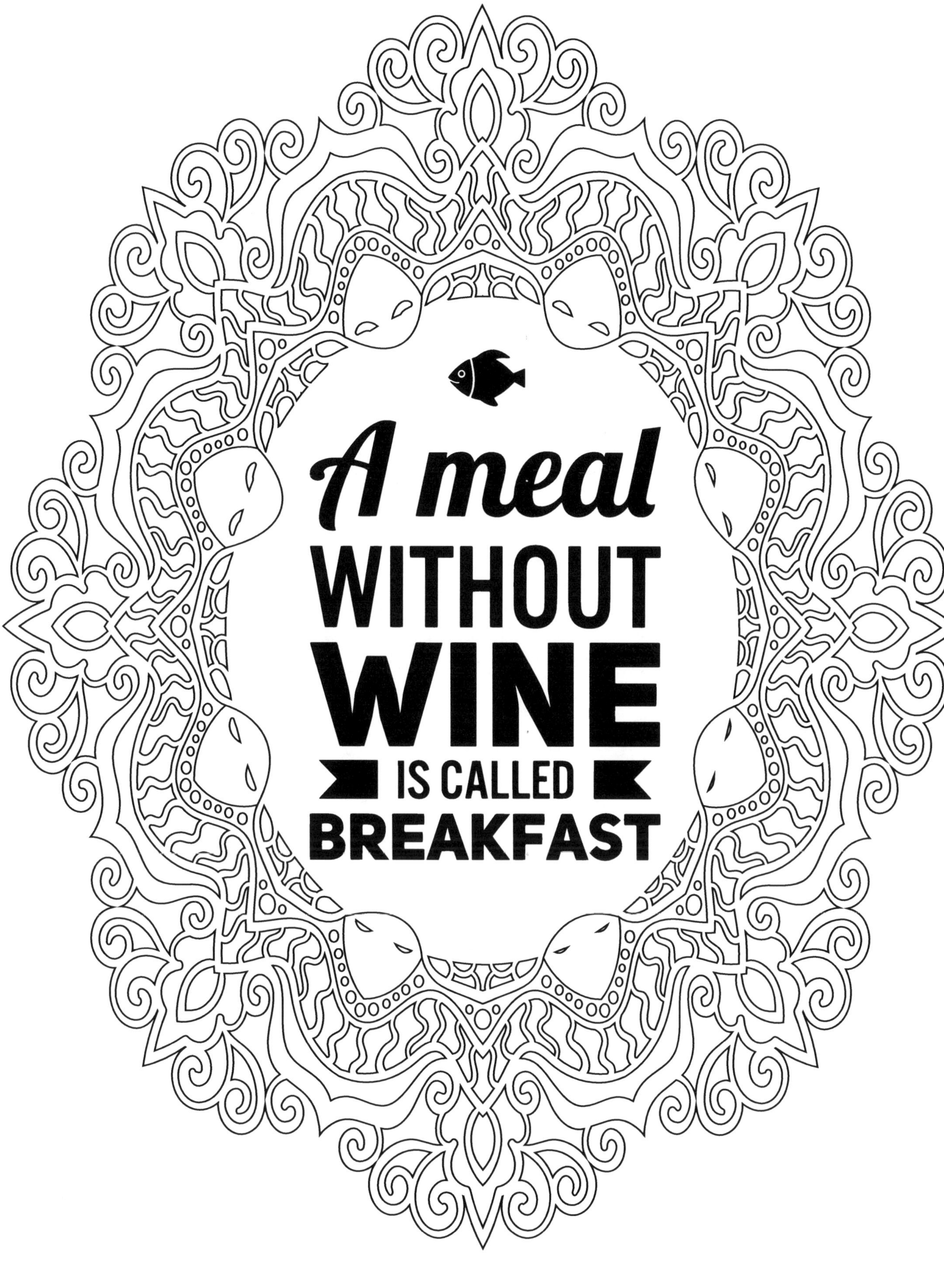
A meal
WITHOUT
WINE
IS CALLED
BREAKFAST

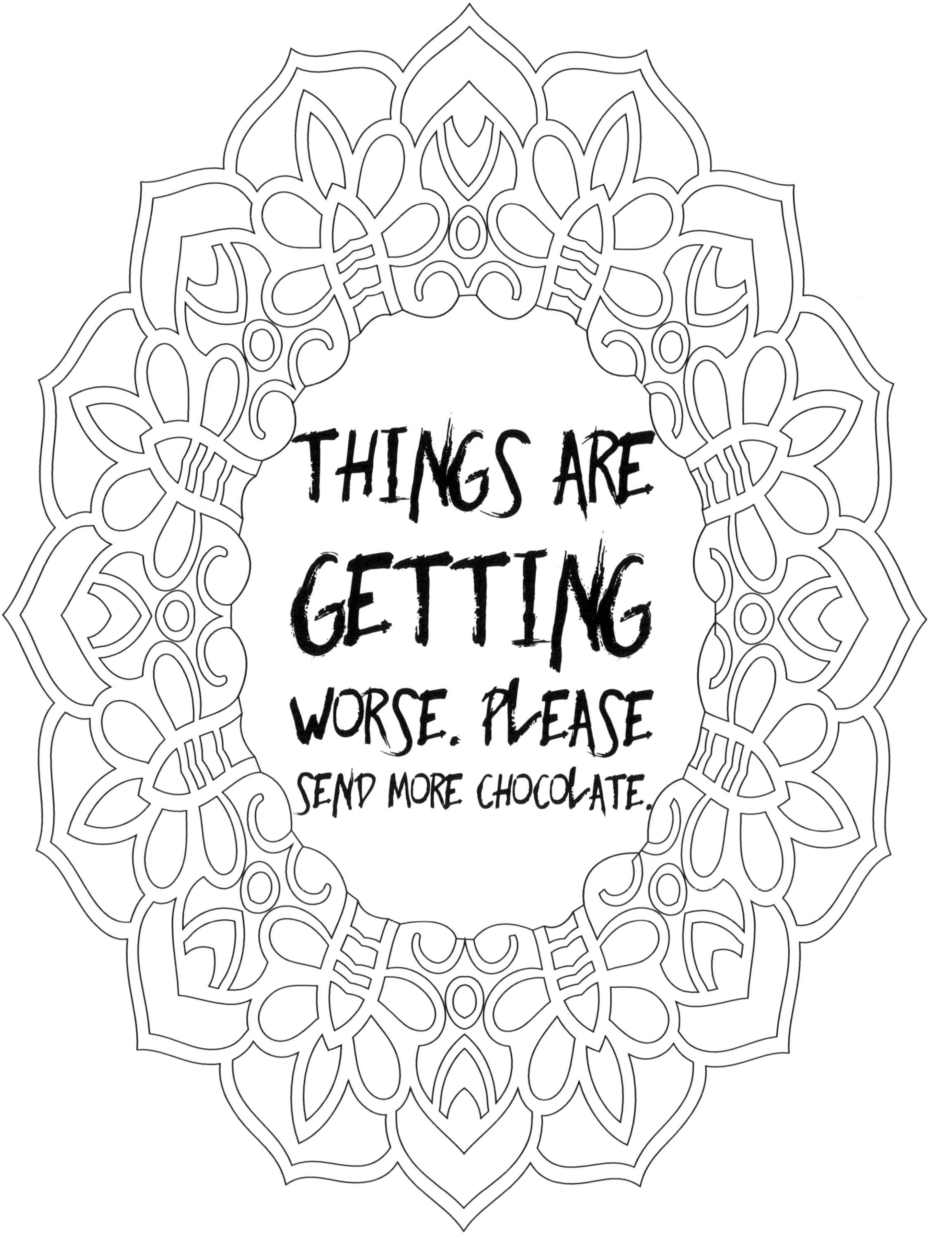
THINGS ARE
GETTING
WORSE. PLEASE
SEND MORE CHOCOLATE.

WHO KEEPS PUTTING VEGETABLES *in the wine* CRISPER?

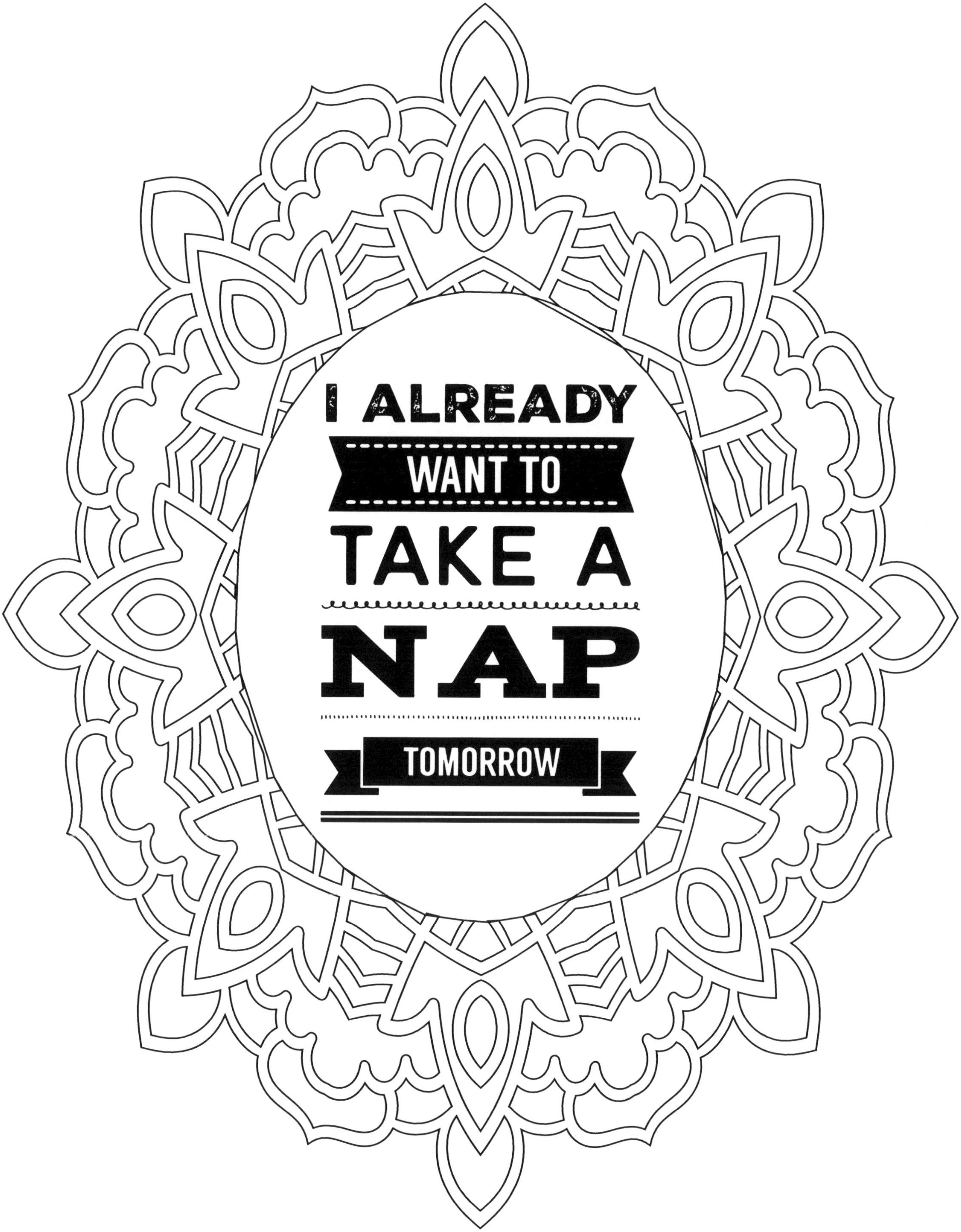
I ALREADY
WANT TO
TAKE A
NAP
TOMORROW

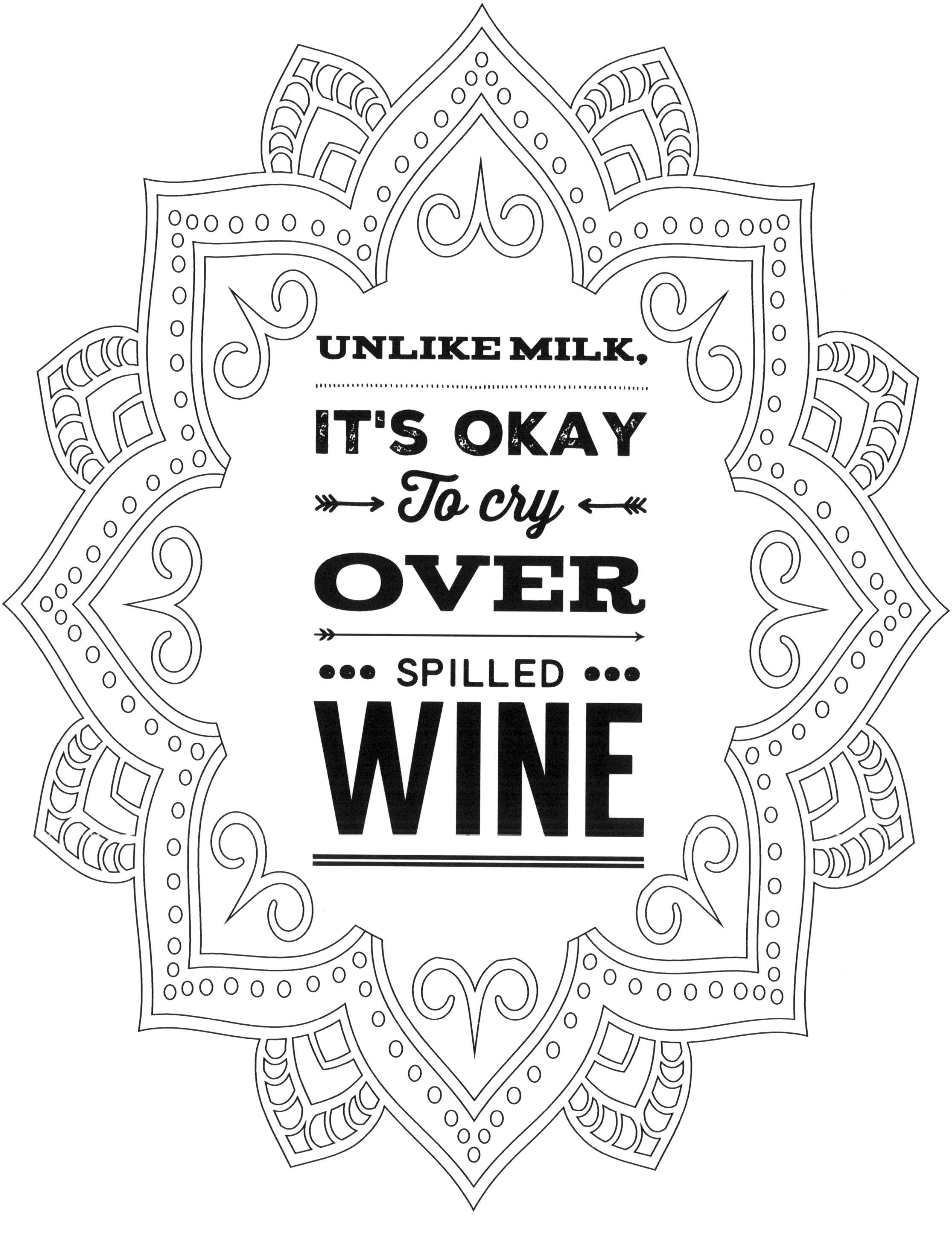
UNLIKE MILK,
IT'S OKAY
To cry
OVER
SPILLED
WINE

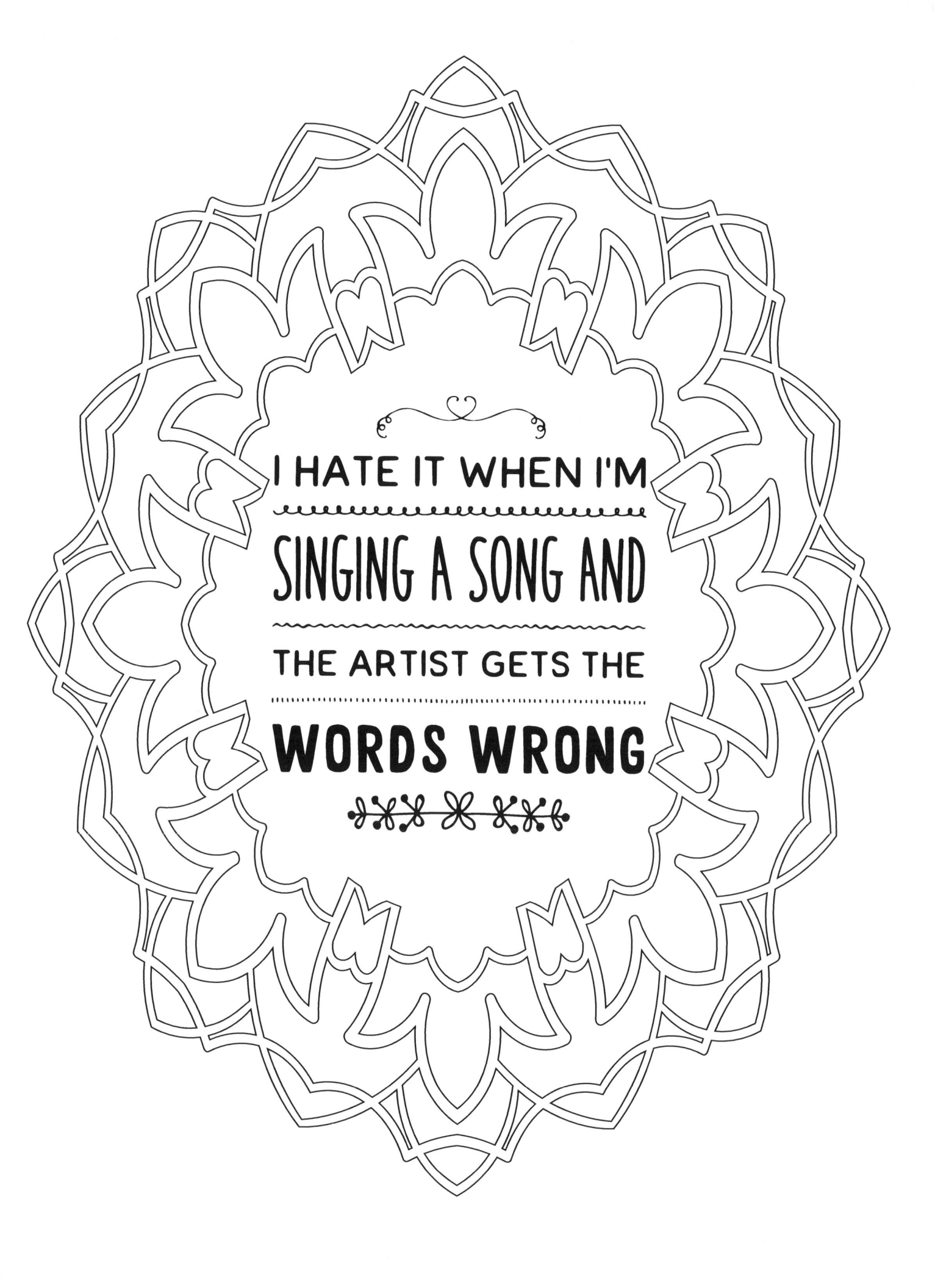

I HATE IT WHEN I'M SINGING A SONG AND THE ARTIST GETS THE WORDS WRONG

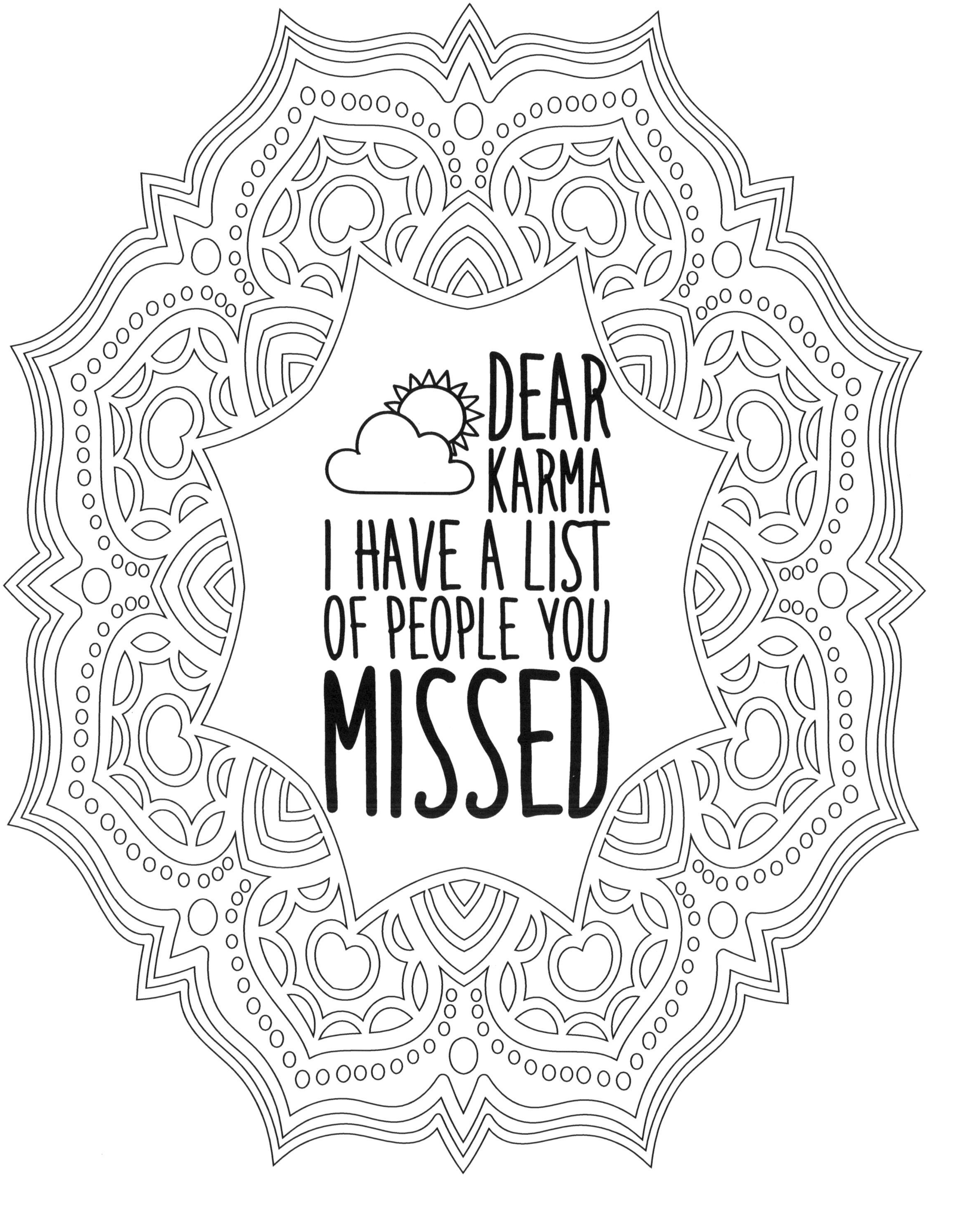
DEAR
KARMA
I HAVE A LIST
OF PEOPLE YOU
MISSED

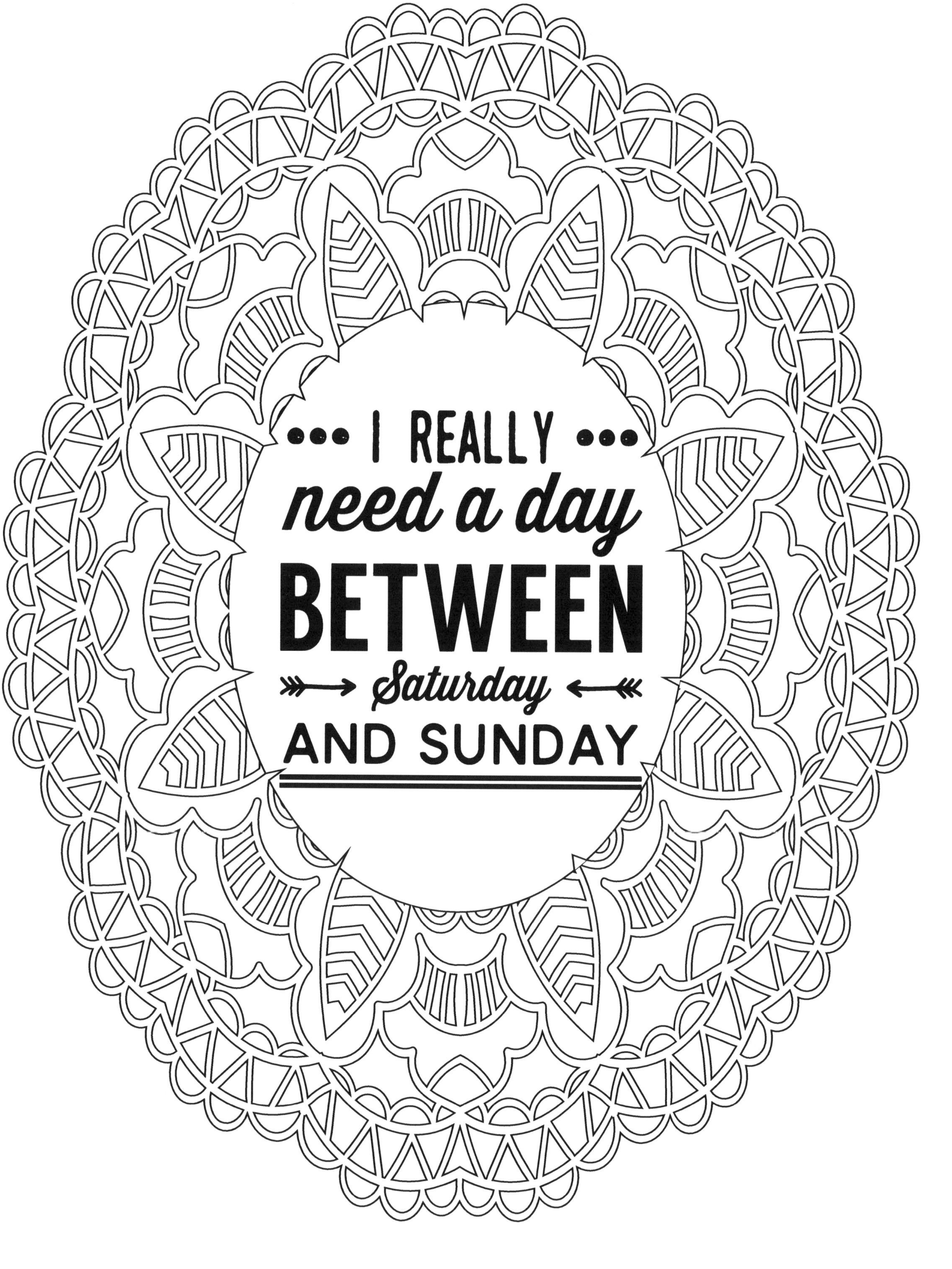
I REALLY
need a day
BETWEEN
Saturday
AND SUNDAY

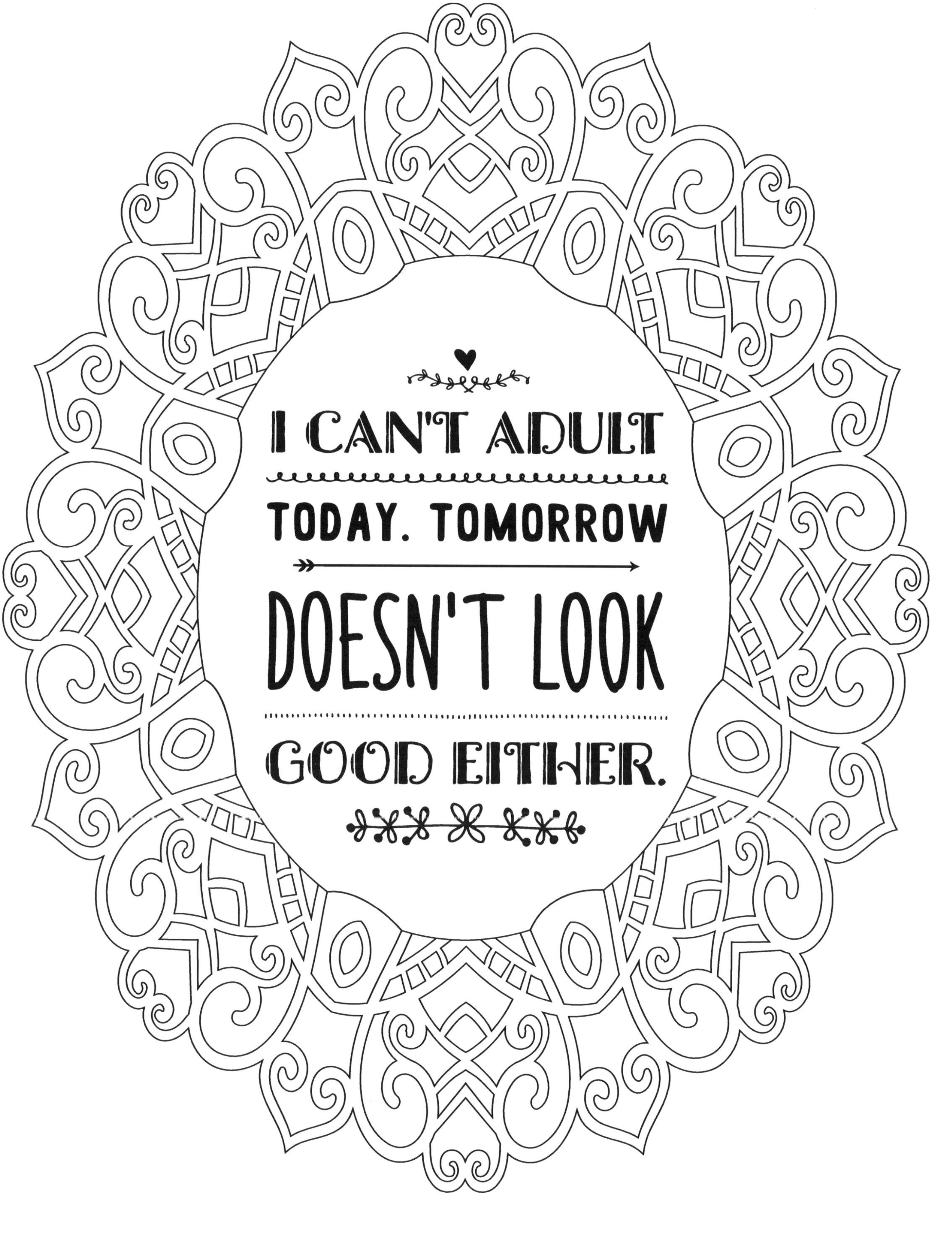
I CAN'T ADULT
TODAY. TOMORROW
DOESN'T LOOK
GOOD EITHER.

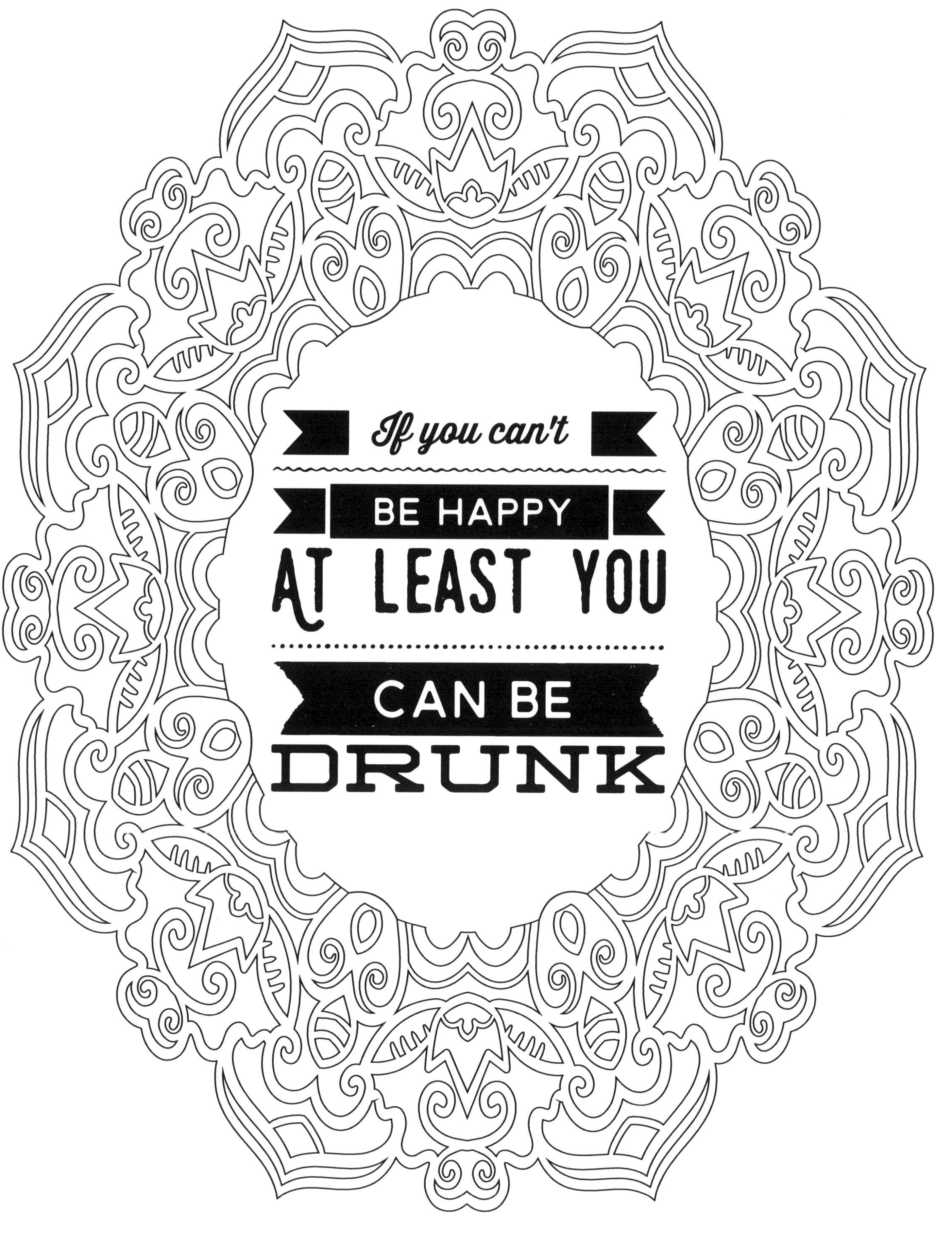
If you can't
BE HAPPY
AT LEAST YOU
CAN BE
DRUNK

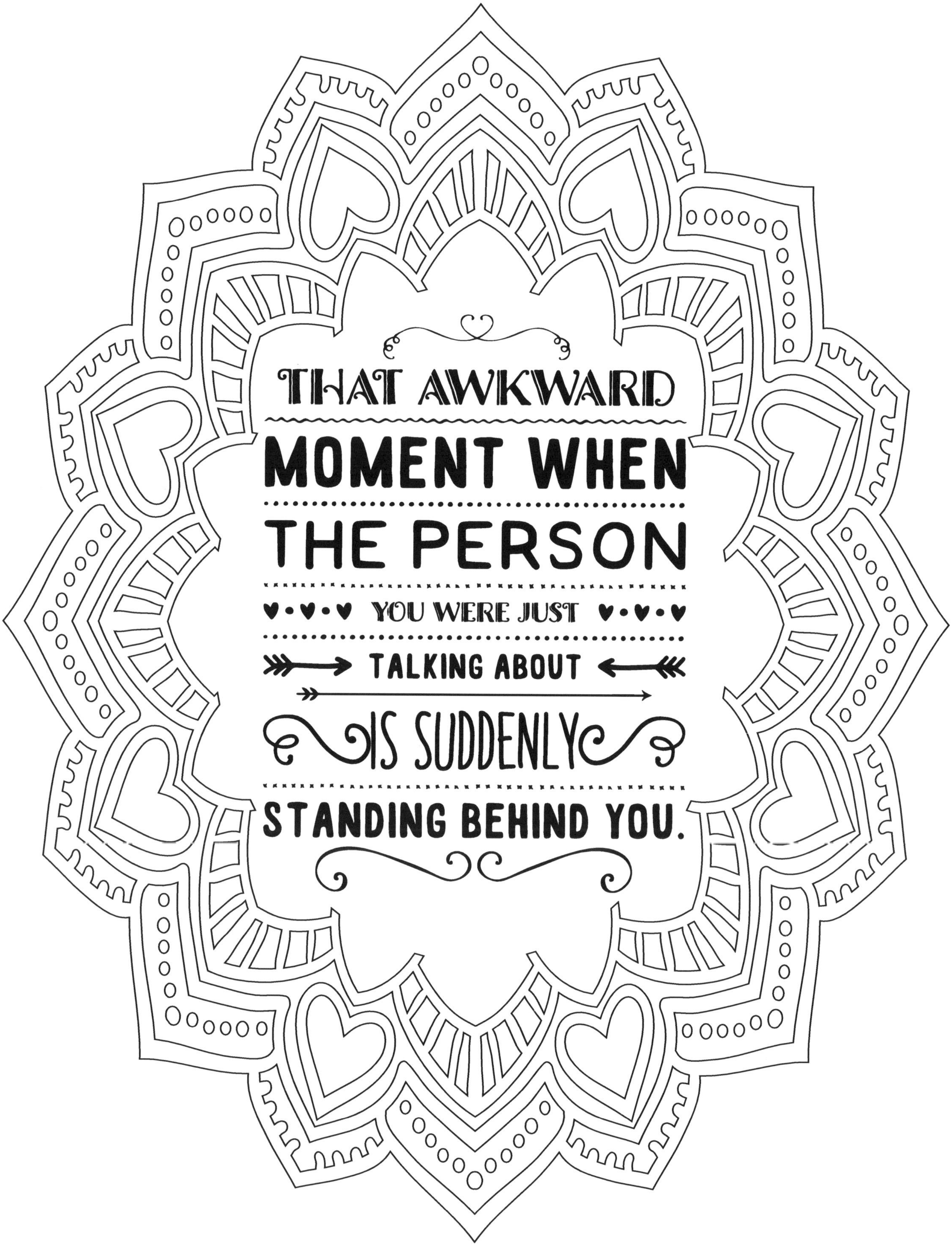
THAT AWKWARD
MOMENT WHEN
THE PERSON
YOU WERE JUST
TALKING ABOUT
IS SUDDENLY
STANDING BEHIND YOU.

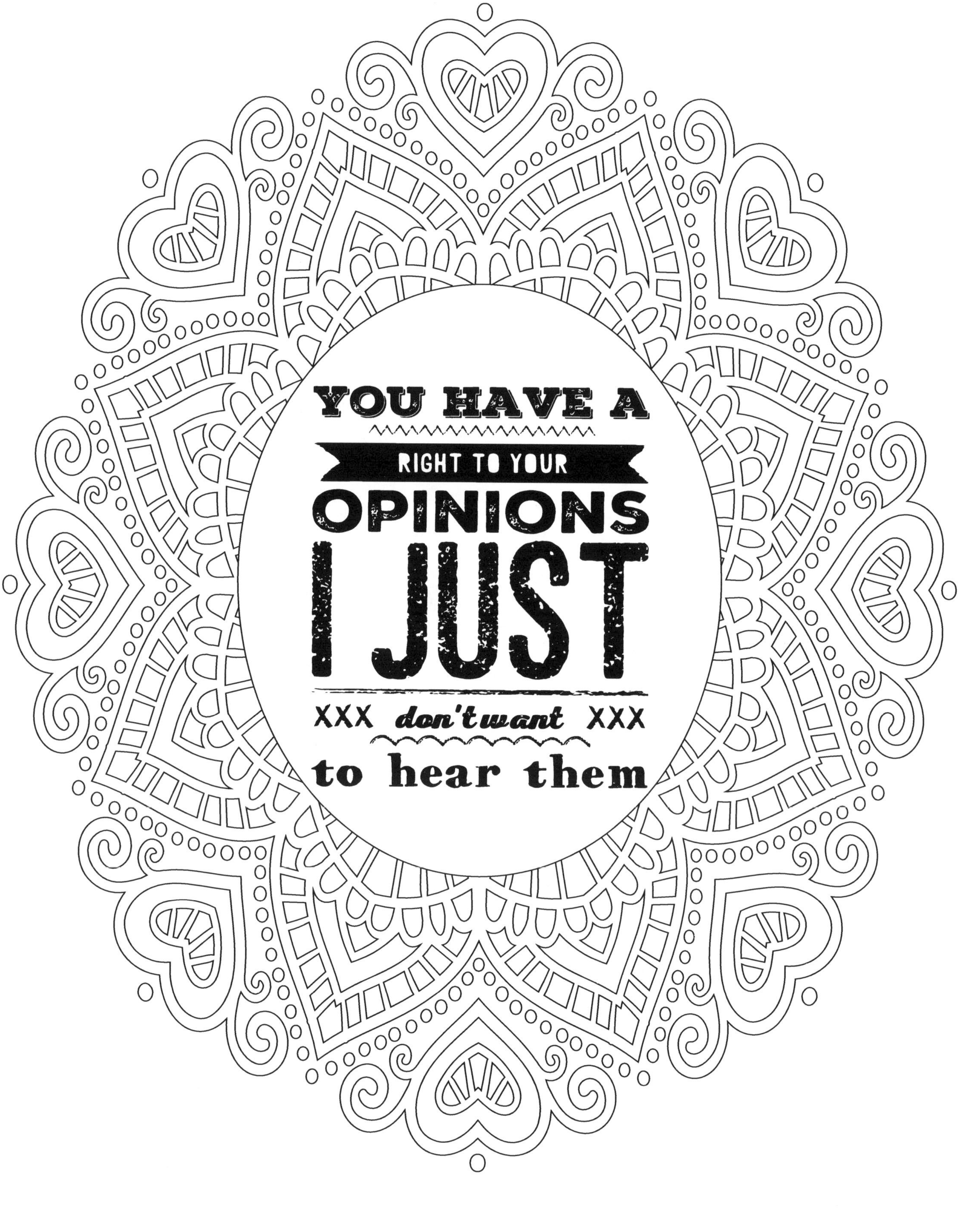
YOU HAVE A
RIGHT TO YOUR
OPINIONS
I JUST
XXX don't want XXX
to hear them

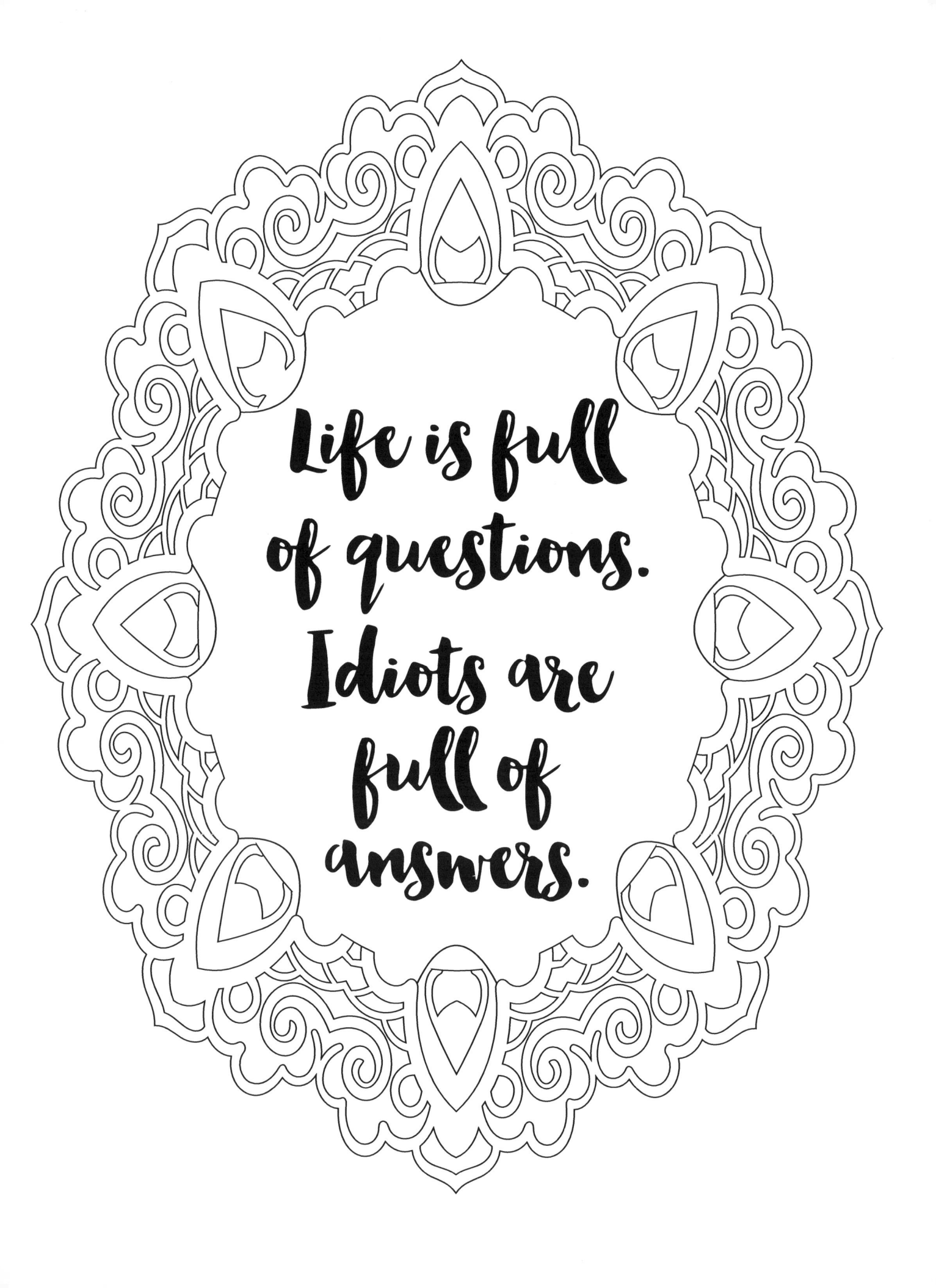

Life is full of questions. Idiots are full of answers.

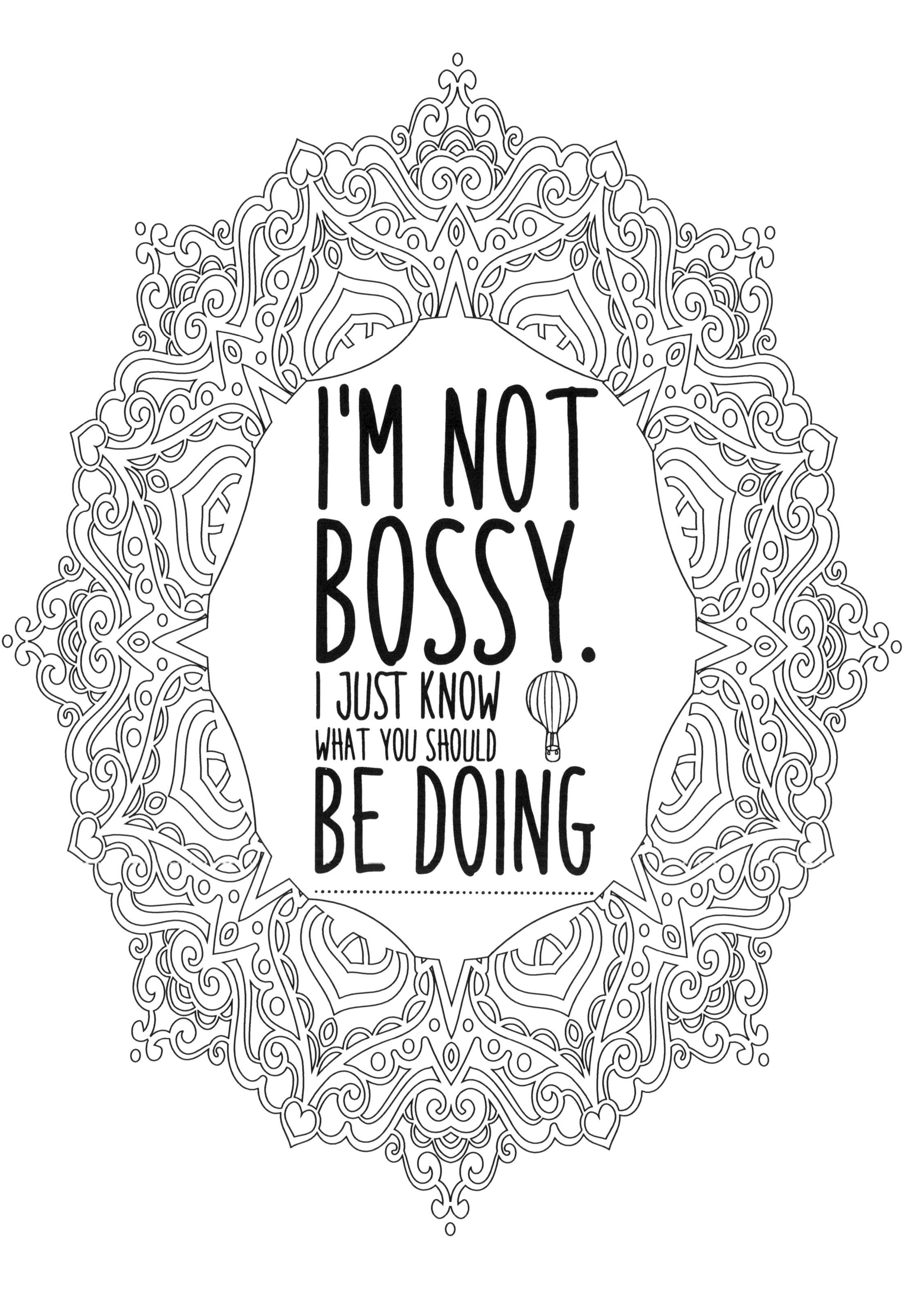
I'M NOT
BOSSY.
I JUST KNOW
WHAT YOU SHOULD
BE DOING

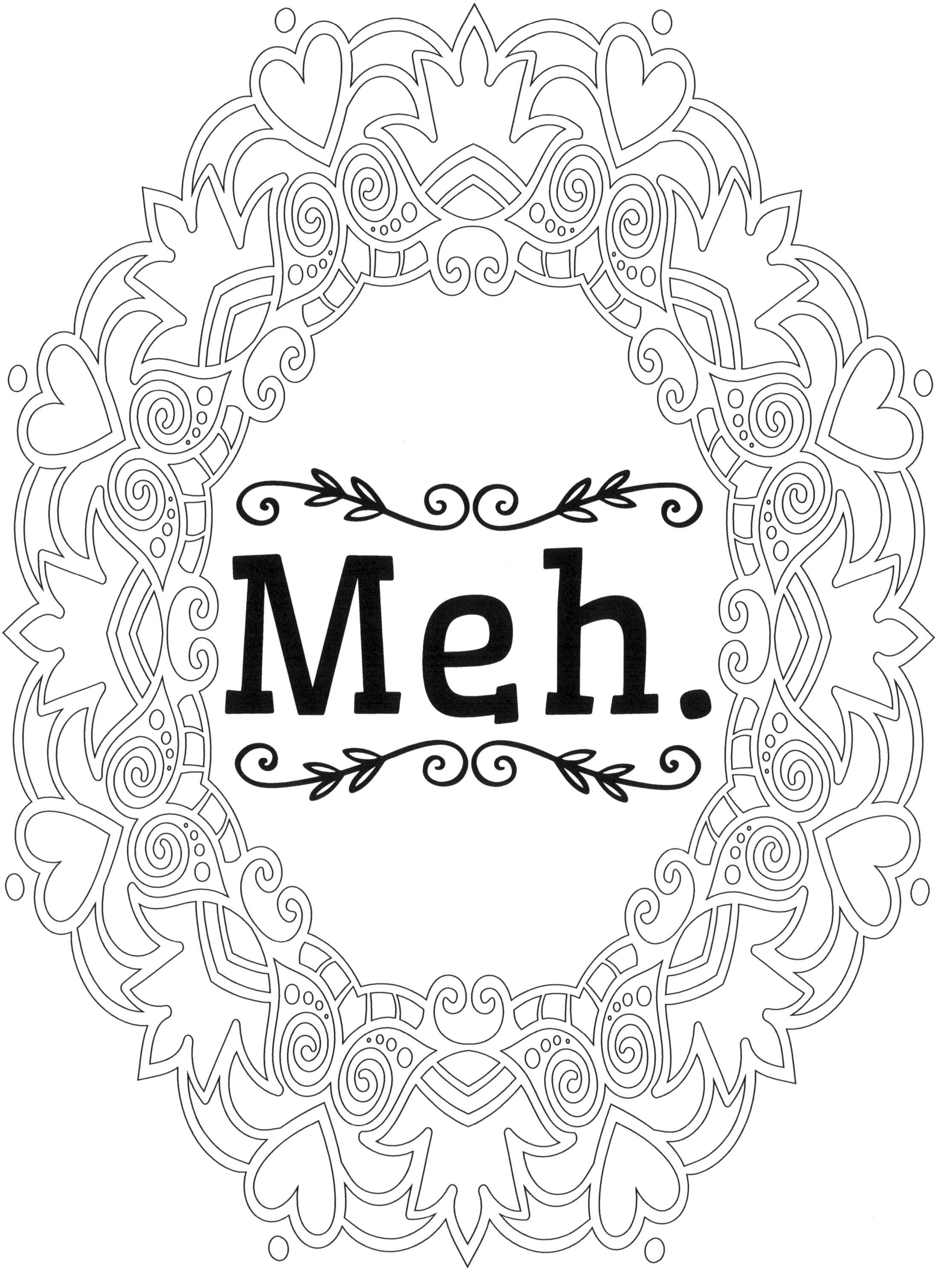
Meh.

HOW DO I LIKE MY EGGS? UM, IN A CAKE?

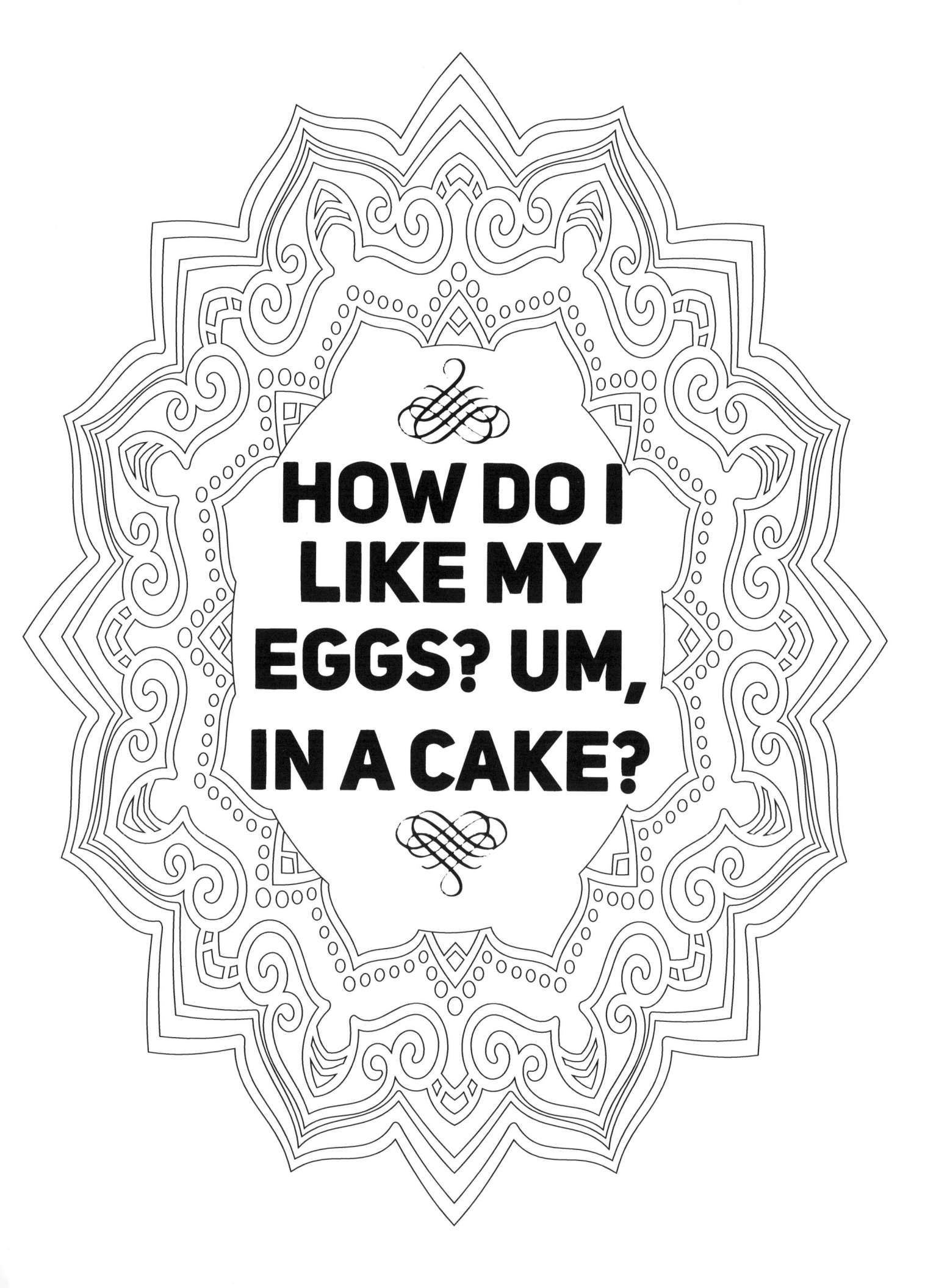

BE SURE TO FOLLOW US ON INSTAGRAM FOR THE LATEST NEWS, SNEAK PEEKS, & GIVEAWAYS

@PapeterieBleu

CHECK OUT OUR OTHER BOOKS!

GOO.GL/vGNZx2

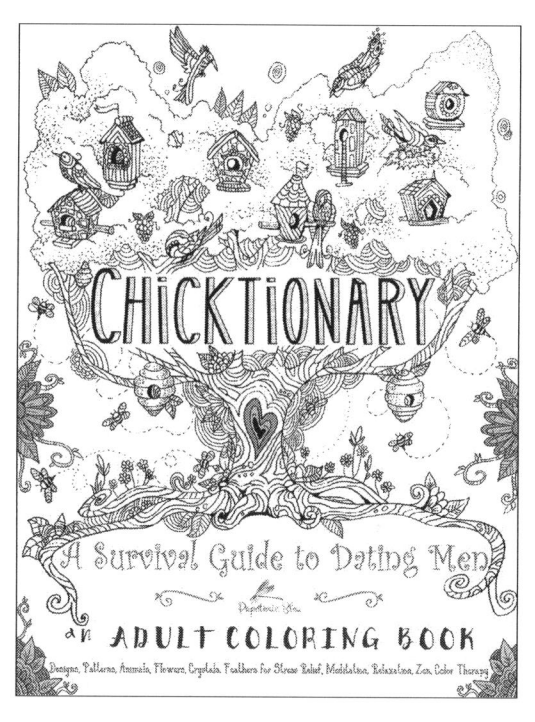

CHECK OUT OUR OTHER BOOKS!

GOO.GL/vGNZx2

#MOMLIFE
AN ADULT COLORING BOOK
MAMA HAIR DON'T CARE

SUGAR SKULLS at MIDNIGHT VOLUME 2
ANIMALS & ALIENS ADULT COLORING BOOK

MINDFUL MANDALAS
an ADULT COLORING BOOK

MASTER MANDALAS
an ADULT COLORING BOOK

MANDALAS AT MIDNIGHT
an ADULT COLORING BOOK

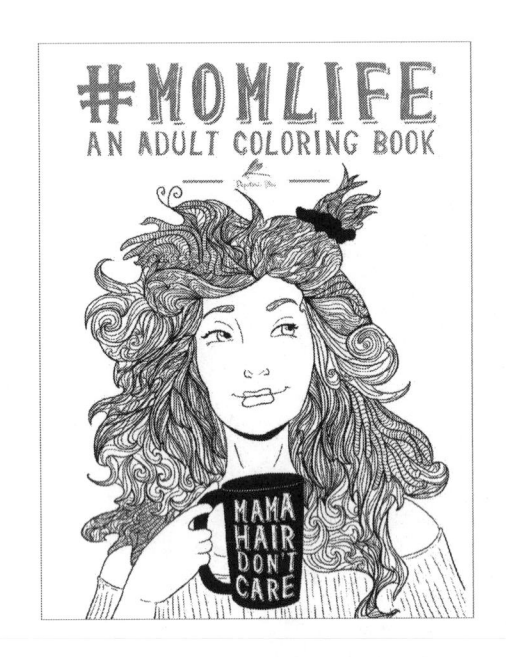

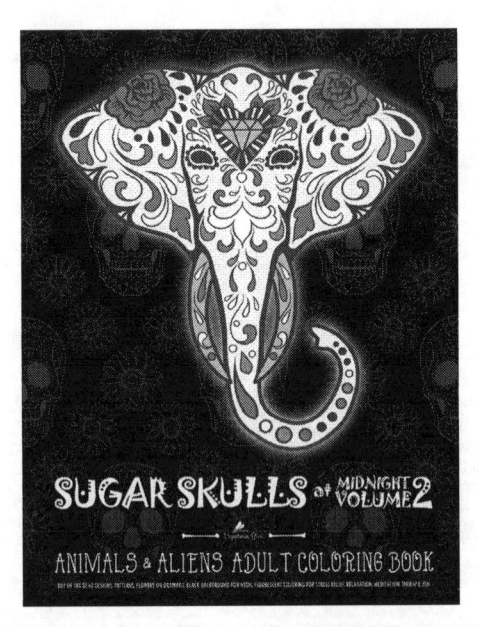

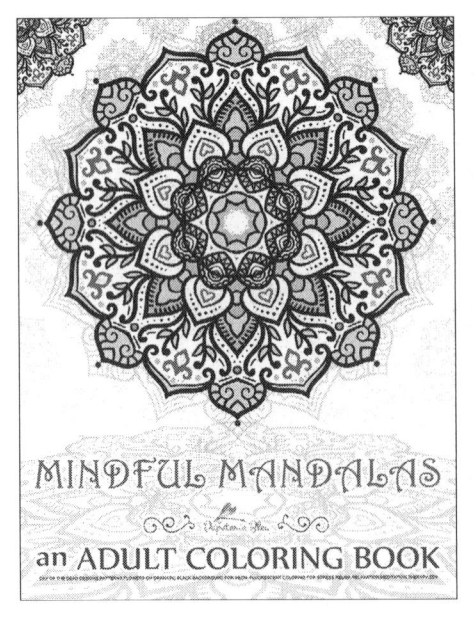

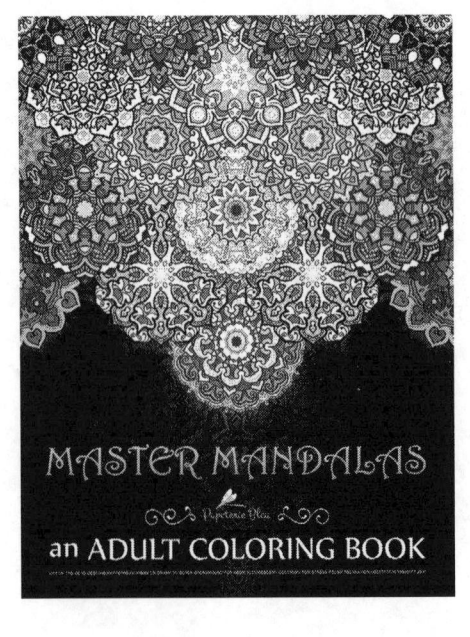

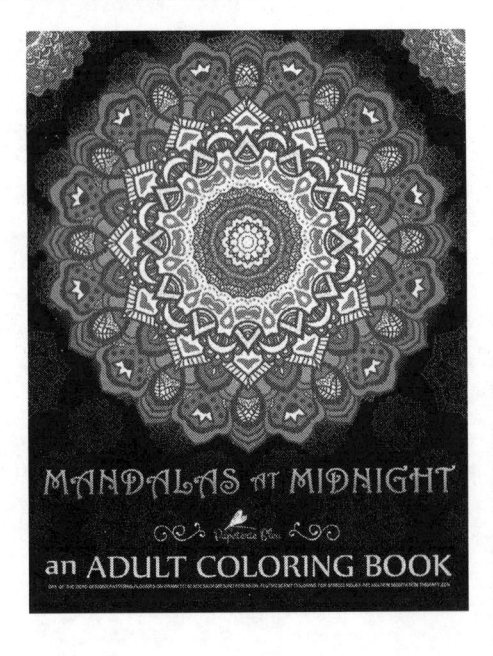

Made in the USA
Lexington, KY
21 May 2016